walking with wisdom's daughters

For the coming of Wisdom's Church:

Her daughters and sons

Walking together

In equal partnership

For the sake of the Gospel.

walking with wisdom's daughters

twelve celebrations

and stories of

women of passion

and faith

Gloria Ulterino

ave maria press AMP notre dame, indiana

© 2006 by Ave Maria Press, Inc.

All rights reserved. No part of this book may be used or reproduced in any manner whatsoever, except in the case of reprints in the context of reviews, without written permission from Ave Maria Press®, Inc., P.O. Box 428, Notre Dame, IN 46556.

Founded in 1865, Ave Maria Press is a ministry of the Indiana Province of Holy Cross.

www.avemariapress.com

ISBN-10 1-59471-063-5 ISBN-13 978-1-59471-063-6

Cover and text design by Katherine Robinson Coleman

Cover and interior illustrations by Jane Pitz

Printed and bound in the United States of America.

Library of Congress Cataloging-in-Publication Data
Ulterino, Gloria.
  Walking with Wisdom's daughters : twelve celebrations and stories of women of passion and faith / Gloria Ulterino.
      p. cm.
  Includes bibliographical references.
  ISBN-13: 978-1-59471-063-6 (pbk.)
  ISBN-10: 1-59471-063-5 (pbk.)
  1. Worship programs. 2. Catholic women--Prayer-books and devotions--English. 3. Women in the Bible--Prayer-books and devotions--English. 4. Catholic Church--Prayer-books and devotions--English. I. Title.

  BX2170.W7U48 2006
  264'.7--dc22

                                    2006007489

Contents

. . . .

"And they recognized him."

"Were not our hearts burning within us?"

"Repentance and forgiveness of sins is to be proclaimed to all nations."

"Until you have been clothed with power from on high."

Introduction

I had often thought that the road to Emmaus was about them. Even though I'd discovered that one of the two disciples on the road was most likely a woman, the unnamed wife of Cleopas[1] (named Mary in John 19:25), it was still about them. Even though I'd preached from the story, somehow it never quite touched me. Until now.

What was it, finally, that woke me up? First came a conversation in April 2004, about that most poignant phrase in the story, "We had hoped. . . . " Followed almost immediately by participation in a conference at Boston College on the Saturday before Patriot's Day, a day set aside to remember the beginning of a revolution. Was it serendipity? Or careful timing of a conference entitled "Re-imagining the Church That Women Want"? In the question and answer sessions, woman after woman spoke up. "We've been doing this for years! Where's the hope! How do we persist in the struggle? How do we stay in this church?" The unspoken words were hanging in the air. "We had hoped . . . that women would be full partners in church by now . . . that women would be ordained . . . that women would be respected, at the very least . . . that the gifts women bring would be treasured . . . that this church would be well on the way by now to proclaiming the gospel of Jesus Christ." Finally, in conversation with a friend over dinner that evening, I was challenged, not unlike those first disciples on the road to Emmaus. As she put it, "Where had I glimpsed Christ in the breaking open of the bread of *my* life? Had I really seen? And was I truly grateful? Well, then . . . name those times and offer them as a gift to others, as a glimmer of hope and encouragement." For we all travel that road to and from Emmaus.

Hard as I tried not to, I had become stuck in "we had hoped. . . . " I had hoped that my love of and gifts for pastoring would be translated into becoming a "co-pastor" of a faith community. I had hoped that the local church would value my gifts. I had hoped that the life I had experienced in church would expand, not contract. I had hoped that ordination would be just around the corner, despite all evidence to the contrary. While I was determined not to become bitter, while I persisted in putting my God-given gifts to good use, it is abundantly clear to me now that I can now go further on this road. I can head back to "Jerusalem," where I belong, just like those first two disciples. I can proclaim to others the glimpses I have been given, by the grace of God. "Jesus, the Christ, is alive!"

Let me tell you about it.

It was February 1993. An invitation came out of the blue from the diocesan office. Would I be willing to serve as a temporary pastoral administrator in two rural parishes for the spring? It would be a four-month appointment, for the time in between priest pastors. I'd been in parish ministry for seven and one-half years, but this was something new. For the first time a lay person, previously unknown to these faith communities, would serve as pastoral leader. It sounded exciting! But was I up to it? After some prayer and discussion with trusted friends, I said, "Yes." Am I ever glad I did! What a joy! The folks were so welcoming. And my ministry consisted in meeting their needs in ways I understood and loved: planning good liturgy, developing a contemporary choir, offering sacramental preparation for children celebrating First Communion and for their parents, providing opportunities for sacramental reconciliation, offering Bible study, leading the Good Friday celebration of the passion. A few special moments stand out. I still remember my weekly communion visits, driving from one house to another and spontaneously breaking into song. And the preaching I loved so much. I had been accustomed to preaching on a regular basis, but now I preached at times alongside the sacramental minister, a priest. And several people commented, "How good it is to see a man and woman up there together!" After one homily, in fact, an eighty-year-old woman greeted me on the way out of Mass. Vigorously shaking my hand, she burst out, "Well, good for you! Who says women can't be ordained!" Of course that was over a year before the Vatican proclaimed that the Roman Catholic Church had no authority to ordain women. Ever! I always realized that this brief time was a precious gift, to me and to the community. But I now believe that this is a gift to all. A glimpse of what is possible in church. A glimpse of the risen Christ in our midst. A glimpse of something more . . . already dreamed, but not yet realized.

The road to Emmaus is a journey of mythic proportions. A journey of call . . . of following Jesus . . . of profound disappointment and loss . . . of being urged to remember . . . of not understanding . . . of being immersed in the paschal mystery . . . of finally glimpsing Christ in bread blessed, broken open, and shared . . . and of racing off to proclaim the good news. Renewed for mission, renewed for Christian community, yet one more time. I know this story, and so do you. For it is a story of our time, resurrection time. And women are to be found everywhere in it, though often disguised through anonymity. They are at the empty tomb. And most likely on the road to Emmaus itself. They are in the Jerusalem community, noted only by Luke as "companions" of the eleven,[2] meaning, all the women who followed Jesus from Galilee.[3] But there's more. The risen Jesus even reveals glimmers in this story of personified Wisdom herself, often known as the Wisdom Woman.[4] It's true that Luke, unlike John, makes little of Jesus as Wisdom personified.[5] And yet, the comparisons tantalize. Jesus, just like the Wisdom Woman of old, appears at the crossroads of intense trauma, profound loss. He reprimands the foolishness of the two disciples, urging them to pay close attention to all he has to say, not unlike Wisdom, who cries out "to those without sense:"[6] "Hear, for I will speak noble things, and from my lips will come what is right."[7] They both instruct, as though Jesus is fulfilling Wisdom's promise: "Happy is the one who listens to me, watching daily at my gates, waiting beside my doors."[8] And they both offer the feast of life. As Wisdom puts it, "Come, eat of my bread and drink of the wine I have mixed."[9] It is the Jesus of Luke's gospel who dines at more feasts with more people than in any other gospel. Indeed, it is precisely at a feast that these two disciples finally glimpse the risen Jesus in all his truth and glory. And so it is for us . . . . companioned by the Wisdom of Jesus on *our* roads to Emmaus.

But if commentators do not generally make these points, how did I come to organize the women of this book around the story of Emmaus? A good question. It all started with Lydia. In researching her, I discovered that her pressing request to Paul (in Acts 16:15), "Come and stay at my house," was only found elsewhere on the lips of the disciples on the road to Emmaus (Luke 24:29), an urgent, "Stay with us," directed at Jesus. Soon thereafter, in a totally unrelated conversation, someone pointed out to me that the words of discovery at the Emmaus feast (Luke 24:31), "then their eyes were opened," were identical to Adam and Eve's discovery of their humanity. There it was again! Finally, the Boston conference, so full of "We had hoped. . . ." set me on the road to Emmaus, once and for all. Did the stories work into that context? Indeed, they did. Why, Jesus even takes on the persona of the Wisdom Woman herself! So come, walk with her. . . and with her daughters.

NOTES

· · · · ·

1. Scholars today generally agree that the person with Cleopas was very likely his wife. She is unnamed, which would have been a common practice, and the two of them were headed home. When they arrived there, late in the day, they urged Jesus to "stay with us."

2. See Luke 24:33.

3. See Acts 1:14 and Luke 8:1–3.

4. The Wisdom Woman first appears in the book of Proverbs, compiled upon the return of the Israelite people from Exile in Babylon, ca. 537 B.C.E. She is a literary device, capable of becoming a religious symbol, to a people who had lost king and kingdom, Temple, land . . . and perhaps even God as well. Who would serve as a bridge

between everyday people in everyday life and a seemingly distant God? The Wisdom Woman was the one: Always the stronghold of the household, she would point the way to the reconstruction of the household of Israel. In time, as in the first century (B.C.E.) Book of Wisdom (7:26), she would even become "a reflection of eternal light, a spotless mirror of the working God, and an image of his goodness." For more on this see Claudia Camp's *Wisdom and the Feminine in the Book of Proverbs* (Decatur, Ga.: The Almond Press, Columbia Theological Seminary, 1985) and my first book, *Drawing from Wisdom's Well* (Notre Dame, Ind.: Ave Maria Press, 2002), 201–208.

5. Nevertheless, the Lukan Jesus does imply that he is a child of Wisdom in Luke 7:35.

6. Proverbs 9:4b.

7. Proverbs 8:6.

8. Proverbs 8:34

9. Proverbs 9:5.

GRATITUDES
• • • • • • • • • • •

• For the courageous women, whose stories I tell.

• For companions in church who offer hope, including feminist theologians and personal friends—both men and women—on the walk to equal partnership.

• For the Women of the Well, who imagine with me how church might be, and who give so much of themselves to the stories of women, yesterday and today: Marilyn Catherine, Princess Fame, Lorraine Fusare, Char Guess-Bardques, Cindy Lazzaro, Mary McGuire, Deni Mack, Melissa Rice, Richeen Smith, and Judith Stellpflug.

• For the gentle guidance and never failing support of my editor, Robert Hamma.

• For the Spirit of Wisdom, at work in the church—God's People—and in my labor of love and joy of giving birth to *Walking With Wisdom's Daughters.*

THE WOMAN
WITH THE HEMORRHAGE

We Rise Up, at Jesus' Command

....

A Prayer Service with the Hemorrhaging Woman and the Daughter of Jairus

• •

This prayer service celebrates a command to wake up. Rise up. Claim our God-given life at Wisdom's feast. The Christ table, or table of Wisdom, is in the center of the worship space. It is set with a bowl of water, a loaf of bread, a cup of wine, and a purple stole artfully draped across it. Tall candles stand at either side of the table. The purple stole—or cloak of Jesus—is symbolic of the healing mantle of Christ's priesthood, open to all. It is purple because it is the color of royalty, and all who are baptized share in the royal prophetic priesthood of Jesus, the Christ. It is purple because it is symbolic of the repentance—turning, again and again, to God who is love—required for all who serve God, including an institutional church grown cold and exclusive. It is purple because, for some, purple is the color of waiting for the promise of Jesus to be fulfilled.

Ministers: *leader, lector(s), the woman with the flow of blood, a woman of today, cantor, and musicians*

Materials: *table, bowl of water, loaf of bread, cup of wine, purple stole, and tall candles*

Gathering Rites

• •

CALL TO WORSHIP

• • • • • • • • • • • • •

Leader: Who touched me?!

All: The gauntlet was laid down.

Leader: Not for punishment, as so often has been the case,

All: but an imperative for claiming women's full stature,

Leader: beautiful to behold,

All: in radiant human dignity, once and for all.

Leader: Who touched me?

All: An interruption, a priority for Jesus,

Leader: an assertive daughter, healed by insistent believing

All: that human diminishment will never do, not then and not now.

OPENING HYMN

• • • • • • • • • • • • •

"Come to the Feast," text by Marty Haugen, based on Isaiah 55, tune by Marty Haugen, © 1991, GIA Publications, Inc.

"Why do you look for the living among the dead?"

Liturgy of the Word

． ．

FIRST READING: ISAIAH 42:1–9, 14–16

． ．

PSALM 98

． ． ． ． ． ． ． ．

"All the Ends of the Earth," refrain I, text by David Haas and
Marty Haugen, based on Psalm 98:1, 2–3, 3–4, 5–6; tune by David
Haas and Marty Haugen, © 1983, 1994, GIA Publications, Inc.

GOSPEL: MARK 5:21–43

． ． ． ． ． ． ． ． ． ． ． ． ． ． ． ． ．

REFLECTION (the Woman)

I had become very small. From shrinking in shame, almost to the
point of invisibility. It was the bleeding, you see, that contaminat-
ed me. My woman thing. Oh, the law of Moses was very clear: "If
a woman has a discharge of blood for many days, not at the time of
her impurity, or if she has a discharge beyond the time of her
impurity, all the days of the discharge she shall continue in
uncleanness; as in the days of her impurity, she shall be unclean."[1]
In short, everything I touched became unclean. And anyone who
touched what I had touched would become unclean. I lived a with-
ering existence. I was a dead woman, walking. In isolation. Not just
for a day . . . or a month . . . or a year. But for twelve very long
years. From people. And affection. From touch, of any kind. It
was a living hell.

My story started out simply enough. It could have been the story
of any woman in my day. Unknown, just like me. Oh, I had my
share of happy childhood memories. That is, until I started to
become a woman, to have my flow of blood. Then something happened to my mother. Maybe she had been hurt one too many
times and took it out on me. Maybe my becoming a woman drew
out her unconscious hatred of being a woman herself. I don't
know. But she would put me down, criticize me at the drop of a
hat. And I never quite knew why. So, when it was my time to

marry, I was only too glad to leave my family home. My husband, you see, was a good man, a rich man. But, we never quite fit. And then the bleeding started. And wouldn't stop.

Until one day, a day that began like any other. I had no idea, at the time, how momentous this day would be. All I knew was this: I was drawn to the water, to the shores of the Sea of Galilee. I was drawn to the water, to the gently lapping waves, like a magnet whose force I couldn't resist. I was so dry . . . from day upon day upon day of empty searching after healing. From year upon year upon year of utter desperation, devoid of all hope. On *that* day, every cell of my body thirstily . . . silently . . . screamed for a healing touch. Then, the next thing I knew, my reverie was broken by a tumult. People descending on the shore. Jairus, the synagogue leader, pleading with a healer from the area. "Come. Quickly. Please. 'My little daughter is at the point of death. Come and lay your hands on her, so that she may be made well, and live.'"[2] It was Jesus! I'd heard of him, this man of integrity, this man of honest words and healing touch. Suddenly, wave after wave after wave of God's Spirit lapped upon the shore of my heart, whispering to me, in an ever-increasing crescendo. "Reach out to Jesus! Touch his cloak! *His* power is of God! *His* power gives life! *His* power will never disappoint! Reach out to Jesus!" So I did. Without a moment's hesitation, until I had to claim my actions. "Who touched me?!" Those forceful words of Jesus challenged the depths of my soul. I already knew that the bleeding had stopped. I could feel the blazing surge of his energy ignite my dead body into life. But *I* had to claim responsibility. *I* had to overcome my fear. *I* had to claim my belief. *I* had to claim my desire to stand tall. *I* had to claim my full womanhood, as a daughter of God.

How odd . . . and yet how perfect it is that my story is paired with that of a twelve-year-old girl. Whose bleeding was about to begin. Whose woman thing would soon be upon her. From young to old, the words of Jesus would stir us to new heights, would simply lift us up to human dignity. "Get up, little girl! Get up, woman shrunk small! Get up off your knees! Get up off your sick bed! Get up from so many deaths of gifts unrecognized, refused, and denied! Get up! Rise up! And let your entire woman-being shine . . . like the stars, for your maker!"

A WOMAN OF TODAY

It has been *years* since that day. Twelve years times twelve times twelve . . . and beyond. And the church that I love has yet to repeat those words of Jesus to women unknown, so many women unnamed, down through the ages. The truth is that the institutional church will only repeat those words when we . . . in wave after wave after wave after wave . . . from twelve-year-old girls to older women shrunk small . . . claim our woman thing. And say, NO! We've heard the voice of Jesus. We've felt the throbbing, pounding of God reverberating on the shores of our hearts. And we will no longer be denied full daughterhood, full sisterhood, full humanity in Christ. Wave after wave after wave after wave . . . we will come crashing on the shore of an institution shrunk small from ignoring gospel values. An institution grown bent-over old under the weight of too many refusals, too many denials of Jesus' life-giving words. An institution grown seed hard, callous to the thunderous calls of God upon its soul. An institution that cannot forever deny the million woman-seeds bursting open the flood gates of resurrection. Wave after wave after wave after wave, we will teach those precious words of Jesus once again, "Get up, little girl! Get up, shrunken woman! Rise up to full stature! For your faith has made you well!"

MUSICAL RESPONSE

"Te Deum Fun Song," text and tune by Colleen Fulmer, in the cassette collection and book *Her Wings Unfurled*, available through heartbeatscatlogue.org, © 1989, Colleen Fulmer.

The refrain is: "Praise our God who raises us to new life, God who does such wonders, Alleluia, Alleluia."

Ritual of Rising Up to New Life

INTRODUCTION *(The Leader)*

Leader: Do you believe that you are a daughter or son of God, made in the divine image?

All:	Yes, I do believe.
Leader:	Do you believe that you are a sister or brother of Christ, one with all who are baptized?
All:	Yes, I do believe.
Leader:	Do you believe that Jesus intends for you to claim your God-given womanhood or manhood, with all your gifts, for the good of all?
All:	Yes, I do believe.
Leader:	Do you believe that God intends for you to fully use these gifts in love, for the honor and glory of God?
All:	Yes, I do believe.
Leader:	Then, rise up. Stand tall. For your faith has made you well. Stand tall and come to the feast of Christ, Wisdom's table. As you approach the table, touch the purple stole, Christ's healing cloak, and proceed to one of the leaders. Proclaim your name, and claim your full stature as daughter or son of God and sister or brother of Christ.

Leaders model for the group by coming before each other and saying, "My name is _____, and I am a daughter/son of God, a sister/brother in Christ."

MUSIC DURING THE RITUAL
• •

"Stand Firm," text is Cameroon traditional solidarity song; tune is TRADITIONAL CAMEROON, arr. by John Bell, in the collection *There Is One Among Us*, © 1998, WGRG, Iona Community. GIA Publications, Inc., exclusive North American agent.

Followed by:

"Behold, I Make All Things New," text and tune from the Iona Community, © 1995, Iona Community. GIA Publications, Inc., exclusive North American agent.

"Why do you look for the living among the dead?"

Closing Rites

BLESSING

Each "half" of the assembly facing the other.

All: You are woman, man,
              blessing,
                   image of God.
         Behold, then, what God intends.
              Labor with God and
                   rise up by Christ's measure.
         Become woman, fully alive,
              partner in equal stature with man,
                   blessing for our world.
         Amen! Alleluia! Amen!

CLOSING HYMN

"Wings Unfurled," text and tune by Colleen Fulmer, from the cassette collection and book *Her Wings Unfurled*, available through heartbeatscatlogue.org © 1989, Colleen Fulmer.

Or:

"Sing a New Church," text by Delores Dufner, O.S.B., © 1991, Srs. of St. Benedict. Published by OCP Publications. All rights reserved. Tune from J. Wyeth's *Repository of Sacred Music, Pt. II*, 1813.

The Woman With the Hemorrhage As Found Within Mark 5:21–43

She's one of so many women without a name. Is that because some might want to dismiss her? How important can she be, if we don't even know her name? Or, is it possibly because her number is legion, then and now? A woman who experiences isolation because of her very gender

---

and bodily functions. A woman who calls into question the meaning of holiness. A woman who reflects a courageous, unconventional form of discipleship. A woman whose abundant wholeness depends upon her faith-filled claiming of her life experience. A woman who invites us into the mystery of Christian community, radical in its equality before God, for the sake of healing our world.

Mark told her story first, in conjunction with the story of the twelve-year-old daughter of Jairus, the synagogue leader. What dramatic power lies in this juxtaposition! The woman has been emotionally isolated from the community for the entire length of the girl's lifetime! The woman has been bleeding incessantly this whole time; the girl is at an age for her bleeding to begin. The woman is alone; the girl has an advocate, her father Jairus, who fervently advocates on her behalf. And yet, both the woman and the girl's father know where to turn, to Jesus. Both the woman and the girl are at the point of death, either emotional or physical. In the end, both are raised to new life by Jesus and restored to community. The woman becomes family with Jesus, as "daughter;" the daughter is restored to her parents.

Both Matthew (9:18–26) and Luke (8:40–56) include the story of this pair in their gospels. But the usually abrupt Mark is the one who offers us the most details. He tells us that the woman must have had some wealth, for she has gone from doctor to doctor to doctor, and has "spent all that she had," only to become worse. He tells us that she has "heard" about Jesus, a sign—for Mark—of coming to discipleship. He tells that there was an exchange of power between the woman and Jesus, immediately following her touch . . . for "she felt in her body that she was healed of her disease." He is the first to affirm what the other two carefully preserve, that she is now a "daughter," and that her "faith has made [her] well." Who is this nameless woman? And what might she proclaim to us?

She is a woman in isolation, almost beyond comprehension. She cannot touch anyone, or anything they might touch, or run the risk of doing either. Why? Because of her bodily discharge, her incessant bleeding for twelve very long years. The Law of Moses is very clear. "If a woman has a discharge of blood for many days, not at the time of her impurity, or if she has a discharge beyond the time of her impurity, all the days of the discharge she shall continue in uncleanness; as in the days of her impurity, she shall be unclean. Every bed on which she lies during all the days of her discharge shall be treated as the bed of her impurity; and everything on which she sits shall be unclean. . . . Whoever touches these things shall be unclean. . .".[3] A woman is unclean as long as she bleeds; she can only become clean again after seven days from the time her bleeding stops. And on the eighth day, a sin offering and a burnt offering must be made as atonement on her behalf by the priest. This woman knows the law on bleeding well. Like other faithful Jews, she knows it is part of the "Holiness Code,"[4] a section of the Book of Leviticus. She knows how her people think. They are God's people, and they must be holy. Which means, in effect, they must be pure. They must fiercely guard against any form of uncleanness. She knows there are four sources of impurity: carcasses, childbirth, scale disease, and genital discharges of men and women.[5] And she knows that she is guilty, and therefore to be shunned, *simply* because of her bodily functions. She understands the reasoning. Because blood and semen are forces of life, their loss means death. And contamination from death is to be avoided at all costs. She understands, all right. She has heard children cry out, "Unclean!" as she goes by. She has been pierced by the disdainful glances of their parents. She has been withered by it all. It doesn't matter that she has not made a bad moral choice. It doesn't matter that she has tried everything to stop the bleeding— doctor after doctor, remedies suggested in the Talmud,[6] even locating and ingesting a barleycorn found in the dung of a white she-ass. It's all a waste . . . of her time, energy, dignity, and resources. And now she is impoverished.

What might she say to us? Might she challenge our comfortable assurances to her that we don't treat people like that anymore? Or, might she point out the people and the places we are only too content to leave on the margins, excluded from the abundance of the wider community? For Ched Myers, it is people stuck in poverty because of policies and practices that support the comfortable.[7] Or, it might be people who are homosexual. Or immigrants. Or people of color. Or women, who still struggle for their full stature in church and society. Who comes to mind for you?

She is a woman in isolation who *cannot* live like that anymore. She doesn't mean to be a troublemaker, but she *must* claim her dignity, her full humanity. So, in effect, she challenges the Holiness Code, the purity laws. She *knows* that Jesus is the source of shalom, the fullness of life. She *knows* that all she has to do is reach out and "touch his clothes" and she "will be made well." So she stretches beyond the law, and the power of her believing heart runs like electricity through her. She is healed! Almost. "Who touched me?!" Jesus commands a response . . . from her. Should she slink away, certain of the contempt of others? But no, "in fear and trembling," she moves front and center, claiming the whole truth. Contempt is erased by the compassion of Jesus. Human need is placed before the law. This woman is no longer guilty because of her womanhood and her bodily functions. And holiness takes on new meaning. To what extent are we still operating out of an ancient understanding of holiness when it comes to women? Where is the evidence that the holiness of Jesus and this woman with the hemorrhage has yet to take root in our hearts?

This woman is a disciple of Jesus, in a most unconventional way. She is the second woman of Mark's gospel to be healed, following Simon's mother-in-law (1:29–31). In that first story, Jesus is brought to the woman by the men in her life, as is deemed proper. But, even here, Jesus breaks through the conventions by going to her sick bed and taking her by the hand, to lift her up. And she responds as a true disciple, by serving others, for Jesus came not to be served but to serve.[8] In this story, the woman with the hemorrhage has heard about Jesus, and she acts in faith on what she has heard, a true sign of discipleship. She and Jesus both break the conventions of their day in the process, but what matters to Jesus is that her faith has made her well. As disciples of Jesus today, how might our faith make us well? What might that look like for us?

Finally, in the name of Jesus who raises us all to new life, we are meant to be a *community* of disciples. Sister and brother of Jesus. Daughter and son of God. No longer in isolation. No longer shoved aside. No longer dead people walking. No, we are raised to new life in Christ. Early on, within fifteen or so years after the death and resurrection of Jesus, Paul intuited this truth . . . and this challenge. Writing to the Galatians, he proclaimed that baptism into Christ released us from the power of the law. For what? For the creation of faith community, based upon the radical equality within God's family. "There is no longer Jew or Greek, there is no longer slave or free, there is no longer male and female. For all of you are one in Christ Jesus."[9] The truth remains. And so does the challenge.

SOME RESOURCES

Myers, Ched, Marie Dennis, Joseph Nangle, O.F.M., Cynthia Moe-Lobeda, and Stuart Taylor. *"Say to This Mountain": Mark's Story of Discipleship.* Maryknoll, N.Y.: Orbis Books, 1996.

Pearson, Helen Bruch. *Do What You Have the Power to Do: Studies of Six New Testament Women.* Nashville: Upper Room Books, 1992.

Tolbert, Mary Ann. "Mark," in *Women's Bible Commentary, Expanded Edition,* ed. Carol A. Newsom and Sharon H. Ringe. Louisville, Ky.: Westminster John Knox Press, 1998.

NOTES

1. See Leviticus 15:25; for related laws see Leviticus 12:1–8 and Leviticus 15:19–30.

2. Mark 5:23.

3. See Leviticus 15:25–27a. Note that the normal bodily function of menstruation is referred to as impurity.

4. See Leviticus 11:1–16:34.

5. See chapters 11–15 of Leviticus.

6. Maria J. Selvidge, *Woman, Cult, and Miracle Recital,* p. 85, and Garrison, *Women in the Life of Jesus,* p. 62, as found in Helen Bruch Pearson, *Do What You Have the Power to Do* (Nashville: Upper Room Books, 1992), 108.

7. See Ched Myers et al., *"Say to This Mountain": Mark's Story of Discipleship,* (Maryknoll, NY: Orbis Books, 1996), 64–70.

8. See Mark 10:45, a key to the entire gospel.

9. Galatians 3:28.

two

𝒥OCHEBED, MIRIAM, AND BITHIAH

We Hand On What Really Matters

···

The gathering space and worship space are filled with candlelight, to give the appearance of a vigil. The paschal candle and a large loaf of bread (on a table) are at the entrance to the worship space, where they will be brought in as part of the entrance procession. Everyone is warmly welcomed and given a program.

There is a table in the center of the worship space, which waits to hold the scripture and the loaf of bread. The paschal candle will be set next to the table by the candle-bearer. And there is a rocking chair on the other side of the table, for the storyteller.

Lois and Eunice will sit on one side of the table, musicians and cantor on the other. All other ministers return to the assembly.

Ministers: Lois, Eunice, storyteller (daughter of the Canaanite woman), and her baby, lector, candle-bearer, two bearers of the tablecloth, storyteller, liturgical dancer, musicians, and cantor

Materials: paschal candle, large loaf of bread, table, scripture, and rocking chair

Gathering Rites

● ●

GREETING AND INTRODUCTIONS BY LOIS
● ●

(Lights are up full.)

Hello, everyone! My name is Lois and this is my daughter Eunice. She still calls me Mama. We just heard from her son—my grandson—Timothy. He was simply glowing about a letter he had just received, praising his faith with enthusiasm.[1] And praising Eunice and me as the ones responsible for his faith. I still remember all the times I rocked Timothy in my arms and sang to him and told him stories of Jesus and Paul and Prisca and so many others. You probably have some of the same memories. So, now, please take a moment and introduce yourselves to the people around you. Welcome one another in the faith we share.

(Lights go down, with enough light to see the music. Music of the opening hymn—see below—begins softly underneath the Call to Worship.)

CALL TO WORSHIP
● ● ● ● ● ● ● ● ● ● ● ● ● ● ● ● ● ●

Lois: We gather to praise the God of our ancestors,

our NOW and our descendants,

All: Who was, is, and will be forever.

Eunice: We gather to praise the God

who chooses to be visible in human flesh.

All: In women who set the Exodus into motion by conspiring for life,

in outsiders who persistently push out too-tight boundaries,

in all who live out and hand on the upside-down ways of God.

Lois
& Eunice: We gather to praise the God of our ancestors,

our NOW and our descendants,

All: Who was, is, and will be forever. Amen.

OPENING HYMN, WITH ENTRANCE PROCESSION
· ·

"Song of the Body of Christ," text by David Haas, tune is TRADI-
TIONAL HAWAIIAN, arr. by David Haas, © 1989, GIA Publications,
Inc.

*The entrance procession takes place, led by the candle-bearer. Following
are two people carrying the tablecloth, a liturgical dancer with the bread
and the lector carrying the scripture. They move around the outside of
the assembly and then come into the center. The candle-bearer places the
candle next to the table. Then the two people with the tablecloth set the
table, the lector sets down the scripture, and the dancer sets down the
bread.*

Liturgy of the Word
· ·

FIRST READING: EXODUS 2:1–10
· ·

PSALM 126
· · · · · · · · ·

"God Has Done Great Things for Us," text by Marty Haugen,
based on Psalm 126:1–6; tune by Marty Haugen, © 1988, GIA
Publications, Inc.

SECOND READING: 2 TIMOTHY 1:1–7
· ·

LOIS AND EUNICE
REMEMBER THE PHARAOH'S DAUGHTER
· ·

Eunice: Mama, remember all the times I would say to you, tell
            me again about the Pharaoh's daughter. I loved it that

---

she adopted a stranger as her very own son! You know, though, it's only recently that I realized, she's just like God!

Lois: I know, Eunice. And I always loved telling her story, too, especially the part about her compassion. Can't you just see her now, making her way to the river to bathe early one morning, just like she so often did? Only on this particular morning, she heard the sound of a baby crying. And she cried out in return, "Oh, we must save this child!" So she ordered her maid, "Go into the water and bring the baby to me." But her maid protested, "You know that we can't do that! Your father has commanded that all newborn Hebrew sons be killed."[2] But all Pharaoh's daughter could think about was this little baby, this precious life, floating on the water in a tiny ark. So she reached out herself as far as she could. And the miracle was that her arms grew longer and longer and longer, until . . . finally . . . she brought him to safety. The words just tumbled out, "Oh, how beautiful you are! 'I will name you Moses because in the language of my people, Moses means son. And you are the son that I drew out of the water.'"[3]

Eunice: Yes, Mama, I can see it now. And that's where Miriam comes in, the other daughter in the story. Remember how I loved her part in the story, too? For Miriam, the sister of Moses, was off to one side, where she had been keeping watch, all night, into the wee hours of the morning. Listening. Paying close attention to all that happened. Judging rightly what might happen next. She was only twelve at the time, and she took a huge risk, stepping up to Pharaoh's daughter with an offer. "I can find a wet nurse for you among his very own people. Would you like me to do that?" To which Pharaoh's daughter gratefully replied, "Oh, yes! I will make sure that he will be safe."[4] So, Miriam, sister of Moses, brought him home to her mother Jochebed, who had so lovingly made the ark for her little son, and for her heart to ride in, as well.[5] Then, two years later, according to agreement, Moses was returned to

Pharaoh's daughter, known as Meroe, who adopted him as her very own. So that is how Moses came to live in Pharaoh's court.

Lois: Yes. And the story continues. For one day, in the crackling of a burning bush, Moses heard the summons of God. Yes, God had heard the anguished cries of the Israelites. And God would set them free . . . with the help of Moses. So Meroe blessed Moses in his mission. But she warned him. Pharaoh's heart was so hard. And he could be so quick to change his mind. How right she was! For Pharaoh's nine refusals to Moses would rain down nine plagues on the Egyptians. Finally, Moses pleaded with Meroe to join with the Israelites. For he knew it was time. He knew that they would all be set free. But, sadly, she simply could not leave. As she fought back tears, she blessed him one more time, "May the God of freedom go with you." And Moses said, "Because you have loved a stranger as your son, I will teach my people to care for the stranger, and they will remember you."[6] I will teach them, "You shall also love the stranger, for you were strangers in the land of Egypt."[7]

After awhile, the people forgot the woman who had rescued Moses. But God remembered.[8] And God "blessed her, 'As you saved Moses and called him your son, even though he was not your son, so your name will no longer be Meroe but Bityah, which means daughter of God.' It is said that Bityah, daughter of God, sits at one of the gates of Paradise, and whenever a stranger is welcomed somewhere in the world, it is Bityah who bestows God's blessing."[9]

MUSICAL REFLECTION
. . . .

"God, Beyond All Names," verses 1–4, text and tune by Bernadette Farrell, © 1990, Bernadette Farrell. Published by OCP Publications.

Toward the end of the hymn, the daughter of the Canaanite woman comes forward with her "baby" and sits in the rocking chair.

THE STORY OF THE CANAANITE WOMAN

Lois: There's another story I love so much! About a woman who pushed her way into the family. And I see that her daughter is right here to tell us . . . and her child . . . all about it, just like I told the stories to you.

REFLECTION
(The Daughter of the Canaanite Woman)[10]

(*Softly singing*) "Hush, little baby, don't say a word, Mama's gonna buy you a mocking bird. And if that mocking bird don't sing, Mama's gonna buy you a diamond ring." (*Humming, rocking a "baby"*) Oh, child, you're sound asleep. And so peaceful. When I hold you close and look at your beautiful little face, there's so much I want to tell you. There's so much I hope you'll grow to understand. Oh, how I wish your grandma was here to see you! She'd be so thrilled! But it's not too soon to tell you about your grandma . . . and about Jesus.

The story begins ten years ago, when I was only ten years old. My mama and I were nothing alike. She was always so feisty. I did admire that in her, but there was something in her that thought she always had to fight . . . for anything and everything. Most of the time I was nothing like that. Most of the time I was a peaceful child. Except, when the demon would get hold of me. Then I would be taken over, totally out of control. I would foam at the mouth . . . and gag . . . and make terrible sounds . . . and scare everyone away. Mama took me from doctor to doctor to doctor. But they were no help. They said it would only get worse, year after year. They said the episodes would come more and more often, until I'd be totally out of my mind. And there was nothing they could do. Nothing.

Now we lived in the hills of Tyre and Sidon, just north of Galilee. And one day my mama started to hear stories of a healer, a Galilean. She heard that he healed lepers and people possessed by demons. That he had even healed the centurion's servant and two people possessed by demons in Gadara, outside his native land.[11] Surely he could heal me, as well! We were Canaanites, hated by the

"They told all this . . . to the rest."

Jews of Galilee, but that was not about to stop my mama.[12] There was *nothing* she would not do to get me healed. Oh, she was a lioness of a woman, my mama.

As it happened, just about that time, Jesus came to our area. It was just the opportunity my mama had been waiting for! As I said, she believed in the power of Jesus. But she was also a fighter. So, the day of my healing began with Mama screaming after Jesus and his disciples, "Have mercy on me, Lord, Son of David; my daughter is tormented by a demon."[13] Jesus remained silent, and his disciples just wanted to get rid of her. But, of course, she persisted . . . even after *he* insisted, "I was sent only to the lost sheep of the house of Israel."[14] She said she saw something, though, in his eyes. Compassion. Then, uncertainty. Was he *really* only sent to the house of Israel? Would his compassion win out? It was enough to change *her*, right then and there. She knelt . . . and confidently pleaded for my healing, "Lord, help me." She had *never* done that before. At first her confidence seemed misplaced. He even insulted her! Compared her to a dog! But, she counted on that compassion, and came right back at him, remembering our pet dog that we loved so much. "Yes, Lord, yet even the dogs eat the crumbs that fall from their masters' tables."[15] What happened next will probably never be officially told, certainly not by his disciples. My mama said that he was so moved by her faith, so won over by her confidence in him, that he knelt down beside her and took her by the hand. It was, she said, as though he had heard the voice of God through her. "Woman," he said, looking straight in her eyes, "great is your faith! Let it be done for you as you wish."[16] And the demon left me forever . . . from that moment on.

I will tell you that my mama was never the same again . . . and neither was Jesus. She was still a lioness, but gentled forever by that encounter. She became a true disciple of Jesus . . . and so did I. As for Jesus, from that moment on, he put no bounds on who could come to the table.[17] Dear child, sweet child of mine, how very important to learn that lesson . . . again and again and again. (*Humming and rocking. . . .*)

"They told all this . . . to the rest."

MUSIC

"God, Beyond All Names," verse 5.

Ritual of Traditioning[18]

INVITATION TO THE RITUAL

Music of "O Taste and See" (see below) plays softly underneath the following:

Lois: Traditioning is receiving . . . and giving. Receiving a living legend, one story at a time, one life at a time.

Eunice: Traditioning is remembering well. The stories of those who went before us, and our own. Even and especially the ones that are wombed and birthed out of darkness.

Lois: Traditioning is bringing these stories to God for a blessing, breaking them open and sharing the food of courage and compassion, wisdom, and loving persistence.

Eunice: Traditioning is living into the legacy of these stories of God's deliverance at work in human flesh . . . resisting any evil that would wipe out, distort, or ignore any of God's children . . . and extending the table of welcome to all God's children.

Lois: Traditioning is handing on that legacy, purposefully, intentionally, etched with our own fingerprints and footprints. It is passing on what really matters, for the sake of the ones who come after us.

Eunice: Please respond "I am" as you are able.

                 Are you willing to seek God's blessing on all that you are?

                 Are you willing to ask God to help you purposefully name what matters most to you?

"They told all this ... to the rest."

Are you willing to break open the bread of this passion for the sake of others?

Lois: As a sign of your willingness to be part of traditioning, please take a piece of bread and pass it on to your neighbor. We will eat together after each person has received a piece of the whole.

MUSIC DURING THE RITUAL
• •

"O Taste and See," text by Marty Haugen based on Psalm 34, tune by Marty Haugen, © 1993, GIA Publications, Inc. *Everyone is invited to join in the refrain.*

MUSIC TO CONCLUDE THE RITUAL
• •

Refrain only, after all have eaten: "Song of the Body of Christ," as noted at the beginning.

Closing Rites
• •

FINAL BLESSING
• • • • • • • • • • • •

Adapted from Psalm 126 and Isaiah 55:12: *Lois and Eunice each extend an arm in blessing as they speak, and then all do the same at the end.*

Lois: We carry the seeds of our tradition in the bread of our very lives.

Eunice: May we bear these seeds for sowing and kneading, for dying and rising, that our breaking open will become a dance of joy.

All: May the mountains and the hills burst into song before us, as we go forth, ready to share what matters most, food for the hungry and bread for the life of the world.

"Canticle of the Turning," text by Rory Cooney, based on Luke 1:46–58, tune is Irish traditional, STAR OF THE COUNTY DOWN, © 1990, GIA Publications, Inc.

Women Connected to the Birth of Moses

· ·

Three women—a Hebrew mother and daughter and an Egyptian princess—conspire to build a bridge of life across a frightening, terrorizing chasm of oppression. Some might name them enemies, the Egyptian against the two Hebrews. Some might assuredly proclaim that such a conspiracy for life could never happen. But happen it did. And these three women would do nothing less than set in motion the events that would ultimately lead to the Exodus, *the* formative event in the life of the Israelites. Scripture only gives two of the three a name: Jochebed is the Hebrew mother and Miriam, her daughter. It would take the rabbinic tradition to name the daughter of Pharaoh. And she would become known as Bithiah (or Bityah), which means daughter of God.

Before going any further, let's set the stage. The time is probably mid- to early fourteenth century B.C.E., for the Exodus event has been generally tagged as taking place late in the thirteenth century. The Hebrews are an enslaved people in Egypt, and have been for some time. It has been perhaps three hundred years since famine brought them to Egypt in the first place, under the care of Joseph. You will remember Joseph (son of Rachel and Jacob, one of Jacob's twelve sons) as a dreamer and a man of wisdom, who was famous for his coat of many colors. His jealous brothers sold him into slavery to the Ishmaelites for twenty pieces of silver, and *they* sold Joseph to Potiphar, one of the Pharaoh's officials.[19] What follows is a twisted tale of retribution, recognition, remorse and reconciliation.[20] In time, Joseph rose to power in Egypt. It was

"They told all this … to the rest."

Pharaoh himself who appointed Joseph as Egypt's guide during a time of plenty and famine. But famine's fingers stretched out, stalking the *entire* known world in that day, propelling Joseph's brothers on a search for food in Egypt. In the end, Jacob (also known as Israel) was reunited with his beloved son Joseph. The Pharaoh invited all of Jacob's progeny to settle on the best land in Egypt, where they "were fruitful and multiplied exceedingly."[21] And there was healing among the twelve brothers. As Joseph put it to them, "Even though you intended to do harm to me, God intended it for good, in order to preserve a numerous people, as he is doing today."[22] All was well with the Israelites. Until a Pharaoh came along "who did not know Joseph."[23] This Pharaoh greatly feared the Israelites, for they continued to multiply. He tried harsh forced labor on them. He tried ruthless taskmasters. But *nothing* could keep them down. So, Pharaoh ordered genocide, the killing of all Hebrew baby boys. This is where our story begins.

JOCHEBED, THE MOTHER OF MOSES

Jochebed,[24] a Levite, the mother of Moses and wife of Amram, already has two children, Miriam and Aaron. Now a third is born to her, a beautiful baby boy. Like God at the dawn of creation, Jochebed pronounces with satisfaction, "How good (*ki tob*)!"[25] But, given the Pharaoh's decree, what is she to do? She makes the dangerous decision to hide him at home for three months. "When she could hide him no longer she got a papyrus basket for him, and plastered it with bitumen and pitch; she put the child in it and placed it among the reeds on the bank of the river."[26] Is it possible to imagine the profound pain and courage required to release such a beautiful little baby into the unknown?

Scripture makes no mention whatsoever of the father. According to Jewish midrash—rabbinic commentary on the text—some of the Hebrew men are going along with the law and killing their baby boys. Not only that, they urge their wives to practice birth control and abortion. But the wives, in return, band together, refusing to sleep with their husbands. So the men divorce them and even sleep with Egyptian women. Miriam, according to this midrash, becomes an advocate in court for her mother and for all the women; in the end, she saves their marriages.[27]

Jochebed's painful decision is rewarded, through the conspiring (which literally means "breathing together") of her own daughter Miriam and the daughter of the Pharaoh. She will be paid by Pharaoh's daughter to cuddle, care for and nurse her beloved son. And though she will ultimately give him away once again, this time it will be into the safety of the Egyptian court.

THE DAUGHTER OF PHARAOH

Scripture says little of her, only this: that she is a woman of wealth and position, since she is daughter of Pharaoh, probably one in a court of many children from several wives. That she is powerfully compassionate . . . enough to break her father's despicable law, without a moment's hesitation.[28] That she is the first single parent adopter in scripture, taking in Moses as her very own. That she—a woman to whom no name is given—is precisely the one who names Moses. "I will call you Moses because in the language of my people, Moses means son. And you are the child I drew out of the water."[29] That she is therefore a midwife, one who draws life out of the water of birth. That she prefigures the midwife God of Israel, who delivers the people of Israel through the Reed Sea, from slavery to freedom, from no people to God's people. And finally, that she is a healing bridge between "enemy" cultures and religions.

But, the tradition asks, why does she—a woman of position and influence—act in such a healing, reconciling way? Why is she willing to disobey her own father? And what becomes of this courageous woman?[30] We don't know any of the answers for sure, but Megan McKenna suggests that she may have been motivated to act by a spirit of solidarity with the Hebrew people. She, too, might have known what it is to be without dignity, for any number of reasons. She might have been overlooked and disregarded, in a court of so many children. Or she might have borne a child that was deformed and therefore unwanted.[31] In any case, she is revered among the Israelites. So much so that in the tradition she becomes known as Bithiah (or Bityah), which means daughter of God. For she images the God of deliverance. According to Megan McKenna, the tradition maintains that she leaves Egypt with Moses and the others, adopting the God of the Israelites for her own.[32] However, according to Rabbi Sandy Eisenberg Sasso's midrash, Bithiah cannot bring herself to leave Egypt. Instead, she

"They told all this ... to the rest."

blesses Moses and his people on their way to freedom. Either way, she refuses to be party to the oppression. Either way, as an outsider, even an "enemy," she creates a bridge of compassion to *the* formative event of the people of Israel, the Exodus.

MIRIAM

· · · · · ·

Of the three, scripture tells us the most about Miriam, sister of Moses.[33] She is remembered as advocate, prophet, cultic leader, and leader of the Israelites—along with Moses and Aaron—throughout their wilderness wanderings. We first meet her as the young, courageous girl at water's edge.[34] She stands "at a distance," watching, judging, discerning what will happen to her little baby brother, as he floats in his tiny ark among the reeds. Her courageous advocacy, boldly crossing religious and political boundaries to approach Pharaoh's daughter, has given birth to the midrash of her advocacy as a lawyer. According to McKenna, she is regarded as the first woman attorney, an advocate for justice on behalf of women whose husbands were divorcing them and on behalf of those who were poor.[35]

We next encounter her as prophet and cultic leader at the Exodus event itself.[36] As prophet, she speaks (sings, dances) on God's behalf. Scholars today generally agree that Miriam is leading the people of Israel in a worship service, in praise of their warrior God, who delivers them from oppression. Such a service may or may not have happened at the banks of the Reed Sea; more than likely, it happened at a place like Kadesh,[37] where the people would gather to remember and make present the power of the God who had freed them from slavery. Dance and the music of the tambourine were two effective means of unleashing this divine power; for God "has triumphed gloriously; horse and rider he has thrown into the sea."[38] Such praise became part of the tradition of Israel, as we see in Judith 15:12–17:2, in Psalms 20:5–9, 68:25–26, 81:1–2, 149:1–4, and 150 (especially 150:4), and in Judges 11:34 (though here the worship of Yahweh is indirect).[39]

Miriam is a significant leader of the Exodus and wilderness period, important enough to be included in two genealogies. But her joyful song hits a sour note with the question, "Has the Lord spoken only through Moses?"[40] What is going on here? On the face of it, Miriam and Aaron "spoke against Moses because of the Cushite woman whom he had married,"[41] and God's anger "was kindled against them."[42] But, Miriam alone is punished; for she "had become leprous, as white as snow."[43] Both Moses and Aaron intervene on her behalf, but God shuts her out of camp for seven days. It is noteworthy that "the people did not set out on the march until Miriam had been brought in again."[44] A feminist reading is suspicious of this story—and any story—that does not reflect the God of liberation. What is going on here? Some, like scripture scholar Rita Burns, suggest that Miriam has been caught up in a much later power struggle, after the exile (sixth century B.C.E.), when the Pentateuch was edited in its final form. It is a struggle between the Levite priests—represented by Moses—and the Aaronic priests—represented by Aaron and Miriam. The Levites were the winners. But, is there also a memory of Miriam suffering from leprosy? If so, what was its effect on the people who loved her? It's difficult to know for sure. But, we do know that Miriam died and was buried at the sacred place of Kadesh. And when she died, the earth itself mourned, drying up for the one who had been so intimately associated with the water of life.[45] Her memory persists among the people . . . and the prophets. The eighth century prophet Micah recalls the Exodus event, led by "Moses, Aaron, and Miriam."[46] And for Jeremiah, God tenderly recalls the cultic leadership of Miriam, without mentioning her by name.[47]

All three women conspired to resist oppression. All three women courageously crossed boundaries that institutions had set for them. All three women refused to be oppressed. All three women took significant steps, one step at a time, beyond their knowing, to set in motion *the* formative event of the people of Israel. They participated in the traditioning of a God who sets people free, for the service of God and God's people.

SOME RESOURCES

Burns, Rita. *Has the Lord Indeed Spoken Only Through Moses?: A Study of the Biblical Portrait of Miriam.* Atlanta: Scholars Press, 1987.

McKenna, Megan. *Not Counting Women and Children: Neglected Stories from the Bible.* Maryknoll, N.Y.: Orbis Books, 1994.

"They told all this ... to the rest."

Meyers, Carol. *Discovering Eve: Ancient Israelite Women in Context.* New York: Oxford University Press, 1988.

Nowell, Irene. *Women in the Old Testament.* Collegeville, Minn.: Liturgical Press, 1997.

Sasso, Rabbi Sandy Eisenberg. *But God Remembered.* Woodstock, Vt.: Jewish Lights Publishing, 1995.

Setel, Drorah O'Donnel. "Exodus," in *Women's Bible Commentary, Expanded Edition, With Apocrypha,* ed. Carol A. Newsom and Sharon H. Ringe. Louisville, Kentucky: Westminster John Knox Press, 1998.

Trible, Phyllis. "Bringing Miriam Out of the Shadows." *Bible Review* 5, no. 1 (February 1989): 13–25, 34.

NOTES

• • • • •

1. See 2 Timothy 1:2–7; the Lectionary leaves out reference to Lois and Eunice, twenty-seventh Sunday, Cycle C.

2. Rabbi Sandy Eisenberg Sasso, *But God Remembered* (Woodstock, Vt.: Jewish Lights Publishing, 1995), 20.

3. Ibid.

4. This conversation is adapted from Exodus 2:7–8.

5. Her name is pronounced *Yo' ke ved,* and she is found by name in Exodus 6:20 and Numbers 26:59.

6. Sasso, p. 22. On page 49 of her book *Not Counting Women and Children* (Maryknoll, NY: Orbis Books, 1994), Megan McKenna says that Bityah leaves with Moses and the Israelites, according to the rabbinic tradition. Perhaps there are two strands of the tradition in this regard.

7. Deuteronomy 10:19.

8. This sentence is the title of the book by Rabbi Sandy Eisenberg Sasso, referred to earlier.

9. Sasso, p. 22.

10. See Matthew 15:21–28.

11. See stories in Matthew 8:5–13 and 8:28–34.

12. In Mark's gospel the woman is a Syro-Phoenician woman. By naming her a Canaanite, Matthew is recalling the painful struggle for the promised land.

13. Matthew 15:22.

14. Matthew 15:24; see also Matthew 10:5–6.

15. Matthew 15:27. According to Helen Bruch Pearson, in her book *Do What You Have the Power to Do* (Nashville: Upper Room Books, 1992), the Jewish people, generally speaking, disliked dogs and did not keep

them as pets; however, Gentiles were fond of dogs as house pets. See p. 82.

16. Matthew 15:28.

17. It is very likely, according to scripture scholars, that this story reflects some of the conflict in Matthew's community regarding the welcoming in of Gentiles. As Matthew tells it, Jesus twice commented that his mission was only to the "lost sheep of the house of Israel" (here, in this story, and in sending out the twelve in Matthew 10:6). However, at the end of the gospel, he commissions the eleven to "make disciples of all nations" (28:19).

18. Maria Harris uses this term in her book *Dance of the Spirit: The Seven Steps of Women's Spirituality* (New York: Bantam Books, 1989) to describe the last step of spirituality as a handing on of what really matters.

19. See Genesis 37.

20. See Genesis 39–50.

21. See Genesis 47:27.

22. See Genesis 50:20.

23. See Exodus 1:8.

24. Jochebed is mentioned in two genealogies by name, Exodus 6:20 and Numbers 26:59. She is a Levite who is married to Amram.

25. See Genesis 1:4, 10, 12, 18, 21, 25. Here I rely on Irene Nowell, *Women in the Old Testament* (Collegeville, Minn.: Liturgical Press, 1997), 49.

26. Exodus 2:3; the word for "basket" (*tebah*, literally, an ark) is only used one other place in scripture, in Genesis 6:14, to describe Noah's ark.

27. See Megan McKenna, *Not Counting Women and Children: Neglected Stories from the Bible* (Maryknoll, N.Y.: Orbis Books, 1994), 43–44.

28. Exodus 2:6–8. She takes Miriam up on her offer to "get you a nurse from the Hebrew women to nurse the child for you."

29. Rabbi Sandy Eisenberg Sasso, "Bityah, Daughter of God," in her *But God Remembered* (Woodstock, Vt.: Jewish Lights Publishing, 1995), 20. Nowell, p. 50, adds that the later Hebrew understanding of his name means "to draw out."

30. Midrash is born out of this kind of attentive listening to the whispers in between the lines. It gives rise to possible explanations and stories, which are faithful to the tradition.

31. McKenna, pp. 47–48.

32. McKenna, p. 49.

33. See Exodus 2:7–8, Exodus 15:20–21, Numbers 12:1–16, Numbers 20:1, Numbers 26:59, 1 Chronicles 5:29 (or 6:3), and Micah 6:3–4.

34. Note that all three women are connected with the water of new birth, which will become the water of deliverance in the Exodus.

35. McKenna, p. 44.

36. See Exodus 15:20–21, two of the most ancient verses in scripture; some scholars believe that the Song of Moses, Exodus 15:1–18, actually belongs to Miriam, as well.

37. Kadesh is the place where Miriam died and was buried (Numbers 20:1). As Nowell points out (p. 54), it is a significant place for the Israelites. Its name means "sacred." It is there that the spies report to Moses and Aaron and all the people about the land of Canaan. It is there that the people murmur, wanting to return to Egypt, only to be told by God that they will need to wander in the wilderness for forty years, a time of purging. It is from there that the final journey into the promised land will begin.

38. Exodus 15:21.

39. In the tradition, praise of a conquering hero was ultimately praise of God, the divine warrior.

40. See Numbers 12:2.

41. Numbers 12:1.

42. Numbers 12:9.

43. Numbers 12:10.

44. Numbers 12:15.

45. Numbers 20:1–2.

46. Micah 6:4.

47. Jeremiah 31:4.

three

THE COMMUNION
OF SAINTS

Friends of God and Prophets

···

A Form of Evening Prayer

···

This is our feast. We celebrate friends and strangers, people of goodness known and unknown. We celebrate holy people of every age, especially women, who have been forgotten, ignored, denied, or misunderstood. We celebrate our coming together as one in Christ Jesus, through the graciousness of God. In Elizabeth Johnson's words, this is a gathering of "splendid nobodies."[1]

This service might become a parish celebration of remembrance. It might take place in November, as is often the custom, remembering so many faithful people who have become God's "friends and prophets," remembering all who have died over the past year, or it might be celebrated at any time, as encouragement for us all (in the Orthodox church, this feast is celebrated right after Pentecost). If this is a parish remembrance service, men's stories can be added, for this service has been designed to particularly lift up the stories of women.

There is candlelight in the gathering and worship spaces, and greeters will offer each person a candle and program. Each person is invited to a large table in the gathering area, in order to write down their own name and the name(s) of any loved one(s) on three-by-five cards, one card for each person named. These cards will be used during the service.

If at all possible, seating in the worship space is semi-circular, so that a communion of "splendid nobodies" is formed. At one end of the semi-circle is the paschal candle. And next to the candle is an "altar" table, tastefully decorated in some of the "stuff" of everyday life, for holiness emerges from this "stuff." It should be simple, with only a few items of significance. (Each community will select what really matters to that community.) The musicians will sit on one side of the candle; and the prayer leader, storyteller, and lector will be on the other.

Ministers: *prayer leader, storyteller, lector, cantor, musicians, voices from the assembly, and candle-bearer*

Materials: *candles, programs, large table, 3 x 5 cards, paschal candle, altar table, and community-selected items*

Gathering Rites

GREETING

The prayer leader invites everyone to greet the people around them so that the assembly might worship as a "communion" of saints. *As people are ready, music for the light proclamation is played through once. As the cantor begins, people stand and the paschal candle is brought in and set in place.*

LIGHT PROCLAMATION

"Light and peace in Jesus Christ our Lord. Thanks be to God." Tune by Michael Joncas, © 1979, GIA Publications, Inc.

Evening Hymn: "Day Is Done," text by James Quinn, SJ, © 1969, Selah Publishing, Inc., Kingston, N.Y.; Welsh tune is AR HYD Y NOS.

"Jesus himself … the stranger … came near…."

CALL TO WORSHIP[2]
· · · · · · · · · · · · · · · · ·

Leader: Heaven and earth, join to worship our creator! Give praise to our God, the one from whom we came.

All: For this is the one who goes before us, making all things new, leaving nobody the same.

Liturgy of the Word
· ·

PSALM 141
· · · · · · · · ·

Text is Psalm 141, © 1963, The Grail. GIA Publications, Inc., agent. Tune by Michael Joncas, © 1988, GIA Publications, Inc.

READING: WISDOM 7:1–2, 7, 24–28
· ·

REFLECTION OF REMEMBERING
· ·

Leader: Tonight we are engaged in holy work. Necessary work. For tonight we remember. We remember and reclaim strangers and friends, people we know and those we don't know, friends of God and prophets, in age after age after age. We tell the truth of their lives. We name any evil that would distort and erase, ignore and belittle their stories, courage, wisdom, and abundant love. We lift up the ones who have chosen survival as a holy path through oppression; and the ones who have resisted oppression, laying down their lives for what matters. We remember and reclaim, so that we may grieve, give thanks to God for their lives, and be more fully remembered into the Body of Christ. We begin by listening to a stranger . . . a friend of Tabitha, a friend of God.

Storyteller: I am one of the widows. A nobody. At least that's how I used to introduce myself. I used to feel lost. Lonely. Forgotten. Of no use to anyone. I'd almost forgotten that my name is Zoe . . . a name I used to love. It means

---

The Communion of Saints   45

life, you know. But, until Tabitha came along—those of us who are Greek-speaking call her Dorcas—I'd almost forgotten. What a difference she's made in my life! Oh, maybe you don't know her either? Well, let me tell you about her.

Tabitha is a faithful Jew, a true disciple of Jesus. Everyone says so. Who knows? Maybe one day even scripture will say so.[3] Why? Because she's so gifted, at so much, like weaving. Not just with fabric, but with the fabric of our very lives. It's the way she treats us with her gifts, especially those who are down and out. She wraps us in the kind of clothing that money can't buy . . . encouragement, peace, and the strength of pure comfort. And she shares the work of her hands with us. Her home, for example. It's become our house church, where we gather for prayer every Sunday morning. So now you can understand how distraught we were when she suddenly took sick and died. We heard that Peter was only a few miles away at the time, in Lydda, so we sent for him immediately. "Come, quickly! We've heard of your great power to heal!" Deeply touched by the stories of Tabitha, he came . . . and restored her to life.[4]

Now, since Tabitha has been raised up, she's more determined than ever to lift us up as well. You have gifts, too, she says. Use them, she says. Believe that you can, she says. You never know how one small deed done in love can bring life. A word of truth spoken to power can make more of a difference than you can possibly imagine. Then she told us about Ananias, another disciple of Jesus. He was just an ordinary man, who happened to live in Damascus. Until he heard the voice of Christ in prayer. "Get up and go to the street called Straight, and at the house of Judas look for a man named Saul."[5] You are to lay hands on him and heal his blindness. Ananias protested! "Not Saul! 'Lord, I have heard from many about this man, how much evil he has done to your saints in Jerusalem.'"[6] Indeed, Saul had approved the stoning of Stephen and was "ravaging the church by entering house after

"Jesus himself ... the stranger ... came near...."

house, dragging off both men and women."[7] But Christ insisted! Saul was precisely the one to bring Christ's name to the Gentiles. And so, when Ananias laid hands on Saul, "his sight was restored."[8] In all kinds of ways. You just never know how God will work! Even through the so-called nobodies of this world. Even through the most ordinary of God's friends and prophets.

MUSICAL REFRAIN
• • • • • • • • • • • • • •

"Restless Is the Heart," refrain and verses, text and tune by Bernadette Farrell, © 1989 Bernadette Farrell. Published by OCP Publications. All rights reserved.

Leader: We now, therefore, remember countless other friends of God and prophets, "Splendid Nobodies," *our* cloud of witnesses. (Each of the following is proclaimed by a different voice from the assembly. The one proclaiming stands.)

Voice 1: We remember Hagar . . . Egyptian, dark-skinned slave to Sarah, surrogate mother, survivor, only woman in scripture to see God and name the God she saw, single parent of Ishmael, mother of a nation, according to the promise of God.[9]

Voice 2: We remember the Hebrew midwives Shiphrah and Puah, models of non-violent resistance to evil, fore-runners of the Exodus.

Voice 3: We remember the women named in the genealogy of Jesus: Tamar,[10] Rahab,[11] Ruth,[12] the "wife of Uriah"[13] (Bathsheba), and "Mary, of whom Jesus was born, who is called the Messiah."[14] Each gave birth in a most unusual way. Each took one step at a time, in the dark-ness, participating in God's plan, in a way beyond her imagining.

Voice 4: We remember the nearly invisible, unnamed young Israelite servant girl, who set in motion the ultimate healing of Naaman the Syrian, commander of King Aram's army.[15]

Voice 5:   We remember all seekers, people of persistence, forged in the image of God, like the woman with the lost coin.[16] A broom was the tool of her hands, compassion the tool of her heart.

Voice 6:   We remember women who proclaimed the gospel, especially the women of Easter—Mary of Magdala, apostle to the apostles, and "the other Mary," "Mary the mother of James, and Salome," and "the women who had come with him from Galilee": Joanna—the wife of Herod's steward Chuza, Susanna, and many others.[17]

Voice 7:   We remember the unnamed prophets, like the four unmarried daughters of Philip, the Evangelist, and the women of Corinth.[18] In them, Joel's words bore fruit: "I will pour out my spirit on all flesh; your sons and your daughters shall prophesy."[19]

Voice 8:   We remember leaders of the early church: Prisca, Junia, and Phoebe, all praised by Paul;[20] Nympha, from Laodicea;[21] Euodia and Syntyche, coworkers with Paul and Clement, for the sake of the gospel;[22] and Lydia, a dealer in purple dye and leader of a house church in Philippi.[23]

Sung refrain only of "Restless Is the Heart"

Voice 9:   We remember Lois and Eunice, grandmother and mother of Timothy . . . and all who hand on the gospel through the power of their very lives.[24]

Voice 10: We remember the persistent widow of Luke, Catherine of Siena, Sojourner Truth, Rosa Parks, and Barbara Jordan, and all who speak truth to power.

Voice 11: We remember faces without a name, lives without an award, people of substance who lived faithfully without recognition, from every race, culture, and tongue. They "bore and birthed, farmed and harvested, fetched and fed, cleaned and mended, taught and

"Jesus himself .... the stranger ... came near...."

protected little ones, related to husbands," lovers and friends, "poured forth unending labor, pondered and prayed, sought their own space and exercised their wits in a patriarchal world, finding their connections to the sacred in the midst of myriad daily sufferings and joys."[25]

Voice 12: We remember our loved ones, whose names we have written down, and ourselves, all God's friends and prophets. As you hear the sound of your name, please come forward, light your candle from the paschal candle, and form a circle of light around our worship space, that we might praise our God together. (*All names are read.*)

THE GOSPEL CANTICLE (*Please stand.*)
. . . .

Text is by Ruth Duck from the Magnificat, Luke 1:46–55, © 1992, GIA Publications, Inc.; tune is KINGSFOLD, CMD, English traditional.

INTERCESSIONS
. . . .

The leader introduces the Intercessions in these or similar words: We are truly God's friends and prophets, a communion of saints, gathered as one in Christ to praise our God. We on earth draw strength from those who have gone before us, as models of encouragement, and they continue to pray on our behalf. With that in mind, we unite ourselves with saints throughout the ages, in sung prayer.

LITANY OF THE SAINTS
. . . .

Text is the Litany of the Saints. Tune by John D. Becker, © 1987. Published by OCP Publications.

LORD'S PRAYER (*spoken*)
. . . .

Closing Rites

Let us pray . . .

For ears to hear the urgent cry of God's Wisdom,

For heart to respond, name by name, face by face,

For will to be totally transformed—never again the same—

into "friends of God and prophets." Amen.

FINAL BLESSING

Leader invites each "half" to bow to the other and extend an arm in blessing.

Left: May we be blessed by the Holy One, the triune God.

Right: May we be blessed by Wisdom,

"a spotless mirror of the working of God."[26]

Left: May we be blessed by Wisdom's prophet, Jesus, the Christ,

Who called and fed, healed and challenged.

Right: May we be blessed and sent forth in the Spirit of Wisdom,

to befriend and become prophets for God's creation.

All: Bless us all, in heaven and on earth, we pray,

that we might form an unending circle of praise,

now and forevermore, to the glory of your holy name.

"Jesus himself .... the stranger ... came near...."

Refrain only, from "Angels We Have Heard on High," tune is French traditional, GLORIA.

Re-imagining the Communion of Saints

. . . .

Several years ago now, Elizabeth Johnson gave a series of inspiring talks on the communion of saints in Rochester, New York. I almost didn't go. Communion of saints? What could she possibly say that could connect with life today? Communion of saints immediately conjured up strangers, people beyond the scope of my experience, like virgins and martyrs, some of whom I would not care to emulate. Little did I know the surprises that Johnson would have in store for us! She offered us nothing less than a lively re-imagining of this powerful symbol! Saints became real people, companions on our journey, prophetic energy for struggles in the present day. And the fruit of Johnson's theological expertise is found in her powerfully poetic book, entitled *Friends of God and Prophets: A Feminist Theological Reading of the Communion of Saints*. With the hope of whetting appetites and drawing others into her re-imagining, I briefly try to capture some of her insights. For Johnson, the communion of saints is an inclusive circle of God's friends and prophets, and she presents a comprehensive history of this symbol, as well as a theology of this symbol for today.

COMMUNION OF SAINTS: TWO PARADIGMS

. . . .

As Johnson reveals, the communion of saints has known two paradigms over its two-thousand-year history. The model that usually comes to mind, the dominant one, is based upon "the social system of patronage, taken from earth and writ large into heaven."[27] In this hierarchical model, God is at the top, like a king, reigning in splendor, with the heavenly host and levels of saints, who intercede on our behalf. For God is a distant God. And men greatly

"Jesus himself … the stranger … came near…."

outnumber women in this model, composing 75 percent of the official church listing of saints. Most of these men are clerics.

But there is another paradigm for describing this symbol, an ancient one, an inclusive one. It is found "in scripture, the early age of the martyrs, liturgy, and conciliar teaching that understands the graced relationships between members of the community to be equal and mutual."[28] Picture this. Age after age "Holy Wisdom" touches "person after person in land after land, situation after situation."[29] And age after age they form a glorious "company of the friends of God and prophets; a wisdom community of holy people praising God, loving each other, and struggling for justice and peace in this world; a company that stretches backward and forward in time and encircles the globe in space."[30] As friends, they are "freely connected in a reciprocal relationship characterized by deep affection, joy, trust, delight, support in adversity, and sharing life."[31] As prophets, they are "moved to comfort those who suffer," . . . "to criticize in God's name," . . . "to speak truth to power about injustice, thus creating possibilities of resistance and resurrection."[32] Such a vision honors the entire community of believers, as "redeemed sinners" who participate "in the holiness of God."[33] Such a vision honors the values of contemporary feminist scholarship: inclusivity, mutuality, the raising up of lost stories of women, and solidarity born out of struggles for justice, even in the midst of differences. Such a vision can function "in a befriending and prophetic way, nourishing women in the struggle for life and equal human dignity and nurturing the church through memory and hope into being a true community of the friends of God and prophets."[34] This is the vision that Elizabeth Johnson puts before us.

A BRIEF HISTORY

The phrase, communion of saints, is nowhere to be found in scripture. But, its roots are there. And it all begins with God, "the Holy One of Israel." The "Hebrew word 'holy' (*kadosh*) means dedicated or set apart."[35] God, YHWH, is "holy . . . the whole earth is full of his glory"[36] . . . and beyond comprehension. "Who is like you, O Lord, among the gods?"[37] But this same God is "bent over brokenness and anguish, moving to heal, redeem, and liberate."[38] For God says, "I have observed the misery of my people who are in Egypt; I have heard their cry on account of their taskmasters. Indeed, I know their sufferings, and I have come down to deliver them from the Egyptians, and to bring them up out of that land to a good and broad land, a land flowing with milk and honey."[39] And the people—God's "treasured possession"—are to remember and keep covenant, to share in the very life of God by caring especially for the stranger, the widow, and the orphan.[40]

For Christians, the holiness of God radiated from the human flesh of Jesus. And by the grace of God in Christ, the entire community of redeemed sinners—called by God, baptized into Christ, and gifted and empowered by Christ's Spirit for ministry—shares in this holiness. Early on, this understanding of God's holiness within the community came to be expressed by the term "the saints."[41] Paul writes to the Christian community at Philippi, ca. late 50s, "to all the saints in Christ Jesus. . . . It is right for me to think this way about all of you, because you hold me in your heart, for all of you share in God's grace with me, both in my imprisonment and in the defense and confirmation of the gospel."[42] Within another twenty or so years, the writer of the First Letter of Peter would confidently proclaim the Christian community to be "a chosen race, a royal priesthood, a holy nation, God's own people."[43] And about the same time, the writer of the Letter to the Hebrews would connect the living community with its ancestors "in faith," who serve as a "cloud of witnesses."[44] Their memory empowers the living for discipleship; and discipleship *must* include engagement with the world for the sake of God's liberating justice.

During its first nearly three hundred years, Christianity was a religion under siege. Roman persecution could erupt at any time. This became known as the Age of Martyrs, the time when certain people publicly witnessed to their faith in Jesus.[45] In doing so, they became the very icons of the crucified Jesus. And in doing so, they provided the stimulus for the two ways of understanding the communion of saints, as described earlier. They are, first of all, true mutual companions in Christ; having run the race splendidly, they continue to urge their living brothers and sisters onward. They release enormous energy among the living for continued fidelity in the struggle by their "lessons of encouragement," in the words of Augustine (who died in 430 C.E.).[46] And the living, according to Augustine, become God's "friends and prophets," for "Holy Wisdom is at work among you, searching for her lost coins."[47]

Indeed, Wisdom's power flows in two directions: the martyrs continue to pray for the living, and the living draw strength from remembering the ones who have gone before. And they become one in their praise of the living God.

This companionship model was the dominant one until late in the third century. Then the paradigm began to shift to the Roman patron-client model, which became dominant by the end of the fifth century, down through the Middle Ages to the present. In *this* paradigm, as Johnson puts it, "the saints in heaven went from being primarily witnesses in a partnership of hope to being primarily intercessors in a structure of power and neediness."[48] Forgotten was the sense of the living community as "saints;" all the saints were now in heaven. And as patrons, they would increasingly become intimate protectors for their clients in need on earth. It was only a small step to look for miracles as part of that protection. Indeed, by the sixth century, it became the norm to seek miracles as a way of legitimizing the veneration of a saint. And the communion of saints, as with all aspects of church life, became institutionalized.

With institutionalization, both paradigms were woven into the fabric of the church. By the beginning of the fifth century, belief in the communion of saints became part of the creed. One bishop explained it to his people this way. The communion of saints comprised "the church," living, dead, and yet to be born. "So you believe that in this church you will attain to the communion of saints."[49] By the ninth century a feast of All Saints became part of the church year, with East and West reflecting somewhat different emphases in their choice of date. By the end of the fourth century, for example, the Syriac church in the East celebrated this feast on Easter Friday, linking it to the death/resurrection of Jesus. But, about the same time, other Eastern churches began celebrating the feast on the Sunday following Pentecost, where it has remained. The link to the fruitful outpouring of the Holy Spirit is obvious. In the West, November 1 became the feast of All Saints, where it now stands, as a link to the end time. Finally, the process of selecting saints changed from one of spontaneity to one of centralization. During the first millennium, the people, in a collective intuition about holiness, remembered and celebrated their saints on the anniversary of their death. After this, it became common for bishops to request that the Pope honor these very ones selected by the people. Finally, with the growth in papal power, especially as a result of Pope Gregory XI's papal laws or Decretals of 1234, canonization came under the exclusive jurisdiction of the papacy. Such centralization has its strengths: assurance of authenticity and sharing of holy persons worldwide, among them. But, there is also a tendency to lift up certain kinds of people at the expense of others. Few "official" saints are married. And women comprise only 25 percent of the list of saints.

This brief history would not be complete without naming two significant times of reform. The communion of saints, like every other dimension of church life, was affected by the sixteenth century Reformation. Generally speaking, the Protestant reformers forbade the invocation of the saints, for Christ had already done the work of intercession. At the same time, they honored the saints for the boldness of their faith and the inspiration of their lives. In 1531, the Lutheran Apology of the Augsburg Confession, for example, suggested that we can honor the saints by giving thanks for their lives, by allowing their lives to be an encouragement to our own, and by imitating them. The Pentecost event of the early 1960s known as the Second Vatican Council recognized the concerns of the Protestant reformers regarding the communion of saints. While Vatican II continued to maintain that veneration of the saints was "good and useful" (in line with the Council of Trent), it made several moves in the direction of the Protestant reformers. For example, the council agreed that discussion of the saints belonged within its document on church (in chapter seven of *Lumen Gentium: The Dogmatic Constitution on the Church)*. And the mercy of a triune God is at the very center of this theology of church. Finally, the council moved in the direction of the companionship paradigm of communion of saints, rather than the patronage model, with all its excess baggage.

"FRIENDS OF GOD AND PROPHETS":
TOWARD A THEOLOGY FOR TODAY
. . . .

A theology for today begins in the drafty halls of the Second Vatican Council. For the Spirit of Wisdom was howling, and she was having her way. Council leaders finally agreed, after spirited discussion, that the church is a mystery, centered in Christ, "the light of humanity."[50] Furthermore, just as Christ is the sacrament of God, revealing God's liberating, compassionate, justice-seeking nature to a broken and broken-hearted world, the church is to do and become the same. For "the church, in Christ, is in the nature of sacrament—a sign and instrument, that is, of communion with God and of unity among all men [sic]."[51] This mystery of the church is first and foremost understood as the People of God, for God has willed to make individuals "into a people who might acknowledge him [sic] and serve him in holiness."[52] Indeed, because of Christ, "who with the Father and the Spirit is hailed as 'alone holy' . . . all in the Church . . . are called to holiness."[53] But this holiness will "receive its perfection only in the glory of heaven, when will come the time of the renewal of all things (Acts 3:21)."[54] At the present time, however, some of Christ's "disciples are pilgrims on earth. Others have died and are being purified, while still others are in glory, contemplating 'in full light, God himself triune and one, exactly as he [sic] is.' All of us, however, in varying degrees and in different ways share in the same charity towards God and our neighbors, and we all sing the one hymn of glory to our God."[55] Furthermore, the living are companions "in the human condition" with the saints in heaven.[56] As mutual companions, the saints continue to intercede for the living and the living are inspired by their memory.

For Elizabeth Johnson, then, a contemporary theology of the communion of saints must be inclusive, honoring the holiness of *all* God's people, including the splendid nobodies known only to a few. Living and dead must be mutual companions, on an equal footing, in a way that is nurturing to all, especially to women, who have so often been subordinated. Furthermore, in today's world, this theology must be open to the entire creation of God—people outside the church, as well as the nature that supports us all. And it must promote "the transformation of church and society in accord with God's compassionate justice and care."[57]

One key, according to Johnson, for unlocking the door of this inclusive companionship model is the multi-faceted, feminist process of remembering. There is the kind of remembering that sets the record straight by telling the truth about people. Mary of Magdala, for example, *must* be remembered as apostle to the apostles (see John 20:1–18) rather than prostitute, which is nowhere to be found in scripture. There is the kind of remembering that recovers lost memory, as in the story of the Hebrew midwives Shiphrah and Puah. These two powerful role models of non-violent resistance to evil have been cut out of the lectionary.[58] And *their* story must be restored. There is the kind of remembering that raises questions about holy values. Few would argue, for example, that martyrdom is a holy choice. But, survival can be a holy choice, as well, as it was for Hagar. *Her* story must be reclaimed. There is the kind of remembering that is subversive, which refuses to remain silent in the face of evil. The many stories of women who were raped or violated in any way *must* be told, so that they will not be repeated. As Johnson boldly proclaims: "memory that dares to connect with the pain, the beauty, the defeat, the victory of love and freedom, and the unfinished agenda of those who went before acts like an incalculable visitation from the past that energizes persons."[59] It calls into question the "omnipotence of the present moment."[60] And by revealing something new from the past, it unleashes energy for imagining the future. All such remembering begins with a suspicion of any passage or story that flies in the face of a liberating God. And it continues with a profound listening between the lines of the stories for any whispers, or hints, of a more complete picture. Until finally, it concludes in celebration . . . of so many holy lives that have been nearly lost to the family, the Body of Christ. Who knows how many of these unknown lives are conformed to the life of Jesus, the crucified and risen one? Who knows how many of these lives will help propel the church and the world to transformation?

In this kind of remembering, hope—that community dynamic that expects goodness from God and longingly awaits such goodness—stares back in the face of death's finality. In truth, we do not know what lies beyond the veil of death's darkness. In the end, as in the beginning, there is only God—the God to whom we can entrust ourselves in the ultimate leap of faith.[61] For, as Paul says, "in hope we were saved."[62] The people of Israel found this kind of hope coming out of the Exodus event, freedom from slavery and for service to God and God's people. And for Christians, it is the death/resurrection of Jesus that *is* hope itself, with Mary of Magdala's bold assertion, "I have seen the Lord!" (John 20:18). Who can forget that a fearful group of disciples was empowered to boldly proclaim the Gospel in the face of possible persecution? Only God could do that!

Johnson returns, at the end of her exploration, to her metaphor of "friends of God and prophets" as the basis for a renewed theology of the communion of saints. And this metaphor has five basic elements:

- a communion of "all living persons of truth and love,"[63] who form "a continuous biography of Christ,"[64]

- their creative fidelity in the course of everyday, ordinary life,

- their connection to those who have already run the race, whose memory offers hope,

- their connection to outstanding ones among this "cloud of witnesses," like a "Milky Way thrown down from heaven to earth,"[65] those whose energy inspires the living,

- and all of the above in relationship to the entire natural world.

In speaking of the ones who serve as models for us, she makes a passionate plea for the inclusion of more women. As she puts it, "It is not just a matter of adding women to what remains a patriarchal master narrative. The challenge, rather, is to reshape the church's memory so as to reclaim an equal share in the center for women and thereby transform the community."[66] Along these lines, in 1990 Archbishop Rembert Weakland imagined a saint for today: a married woman, with children, who gives her life in the exercise of her everyday work of reconciliation.[67]

In the end, Johnson says, the symbol of the communion of saints must be expansive enough to include "the primordial sacrament, the sacred earth itself."[68] For *everything* gives praise to our Maker. And it must sing! In praise of the God whose song first set the universe into motion.

NOTES
· · · · ·

1. Elizabeth A. Johnson, *Friends of God and Prophets: A Feminist Theological Reading of the Communion of Saints* (New York: The Continuum Publishing Company, 1998), 8. I gratefully acknowledge this faith-filled theologian, who has inspired this entire worship service by her unveiling of the communion of saints for us today. I have borrowed her phrase, "splendid nobodies," referring to countless women and men, age after age, who witnessed to their faith.

"Jesus himself ... the stranger ... came near...."

2. The words of this Call to Worship are adapted from the hymn "Heaven and Earth," © 1995, Iona Community. GIA Publications, Inc., exclusive North American agent.

3. In Acts 9:36 she is called a disciple, the only woman so named in all of Scripture.

4. See Acts 9:36–43.

5. See Acts 9:11.

6. See Acts 9:13.

7. See Acts 8:3.

8. See Acts 9:18.

9. See Genesis 16:1–16; 21:8–21.

10. See Genesis, chapter 38.

11. See Joshua, chapter 2 and 6:22–25.

12. See the Book of Ruth.

13. See 2 Samuel 11:1–12:25; 1 Kings 1:11–2:22.

14. See Matthew 1:16. All these women are found in Matthew's genealogy of Jesus, 1:1–17.

15. See 2 Kings 5:1–19.

16. See Luke 15:1–3, 8–10.

17. See Matthew 28:1, Mark 16:1, Luke 23:55 and Luke 8:3. Mary of Magdala is found in all accounts; in John she is alone among the women.

18. See Acts 21:8–9; 1 Corinthians 11:5.

19. See Joel 2:28a, b.

20. See Romans 16:1–7. Prisca and her husband Aquila were coworkers with Paul and leaders of house churches in Rome, Corinth, and Ephesus; Phoebe was deacon in Cenchrae; and Junia was named "outstanding among the apostles."

21. See Colossians 4:15.

22. See Philippians 4:2–3.

23. See Acts of the Apostles 16:11–15, 40.

24. See 2 Timothy 1:3–5.

25. Johnson, p. 157.

26. Wisdom 7:26b.

27. Johnson, p. 2.

28. Johnson, pp. 2–3.

29. Johnson, p. 41.

30. Ibid. Johnson has been inspired by Wisdom 7:27 for her re-visioning of this symbol: Although she [Wisdom/Sophia] is but one, she can do all things, and while remaining in herself, she renews all things; in every generation she passes into holy souls and makes them friends of God, and prophets.

31. Ibid.

32. Ibid.

33. Johnson, p. 2.

34. Johnson, p. 3.

35. Johnson, p. 50.

36. Isaiah 6:3.

37. Exodus 15:11.

38. Johnson, p. 54.

39. Exodus 3:7–8.

40. Exodus 19:1–6; Deuteronomy 10:17–19.

41. Johnson notes on p. 60 that, although this term can refer "to the angels, to pious Jews who have already died, or to Christians who die under persecution," it is used most often—some sixty times—to refer to the Christian community as a whole.

42. See Philippians 1:1, 7.

43. 1 Peter 2:9.

44. Hebrews 11:1–12:2. This letter was written sometime between the early 60s and the year 95.

45. The Greek word μαρτυρεο (*martyreo*) means "to bear witness."

46. Augustine, *The Works of Saint Augustine: A Translation for the Twenty-First Century*, part 3: *Sermons*, 10 vols., ed. John Rotelle, trans. and notes by Edmund Hill (Hyde Park, N.Y.: New City Press, 1990–95): Sermon 273.2 (8:17), as found in Johnson, p. 82.

47. Johnson, p. 81; this is one of many images used by Augustine.

48. Johnson, p. 86.

49. Johnson, p. 95, makes reference to a commentary on the Apostles' Creed by Nicetas, bishop of Remesiana in J.N.D. Kelly, *Early Christian Creeds*, 3rd ed. (London: Longman, 1972), 391. Johnson traces the several levels of meaning in the term communion of saints in pp. 94–97. In the West, the meaning was a personal one, referring to individuals or the wider church. In the East, the meaning included participation in the holy things (i.e. the eucharistic elements). As she points out, both meanings are worthy of being explored further today. For example, it would be possible to include the created world in the "holy things" of God.

50. *Lumen Gentium* (light of humanity) is the title of the Vatican II *Dogmatic Constitution on the Church* of 21 November 1964. Its opening statement is "Christ is the light of humanity." See *Vatican Council II: The Conciliar and Post Conciliar Documents.* gen. ed., Austin Flannery, O.P., (Northport, N.Y.: Costello Publishing Company, 1975), chapter I, #1, p. 350; hereafter referred to as *Lumen*.

51. Ibid. It should be noted that the documents were written before an awareness of inclusive language.

"Jesus himself … the stranger … came near…."

52. *Lumen*, chapter II, #9, p. 359.

53. *Lumen*, chapter 5, #39, p. 396.

54. *Lumen*, chapter 7, #48, p. 407.

55. *Lumen*, chapter 7, #49, p. 409; the quote within the quote is from the Council of Florence, *Decretum pro Graecis, Denz*, 693 (1305).

56. *Lumen*, chapter 7, #50, p. 411.

57. Johnson, p. 141.

58. See their story in Exodus 1:8–20. See Reading 1 for Monday of the Fifteenth week of the year, Year 1.

59. Johnson, p. 165.

60. Ibid.

61. Johnson has written a powerful chapter on "the darkness of death," outlining some contemporary theology in this area.

62. See Romans 8:24.

63. Johnson, p. 220.

64. Johnson, p. 225.

65. Johnson, p. 239. This phrase comes from Paulinus and is cited by Peter Brown, "The Saint as Exemplar in Late Antiquity," in John Stratton Hawley (ed.), *Saints and Virtue*, University of California Press, 1987, 6 (see chapter 1, n. 15).

66. Johnson, p. 235.

67. Rembert Weakland, "Story of a Saint of the 1990s," *Origins* 19, 33 (January 18, 1990): 535. Johnson makes reference to this homily on pp. 231–32.

68. Johnson, p. 241.

𝓛YDIA

We Seek Wisdom,
the Face of the Living God

··

This service is a witness to the truth that we humans seek after the living God because it is God who has first sought us out. It is a celebration of God's grace, offered at every turn in our lives. For us as Christians, it is a celebration of our desire to follow in the footsteps of Jesus, the human face of God.

Central to the worship space is a table, with two-foot-long purple ribbons artfully arranged on it. In the midst of these ribbons (enough for every participant) are a glass bowl of water and some greenery, symbolic of our baptism into abundant life. On one side is a lectern with the scripture and a chair for the leader; on the other side is the area for musicians. People are greeted warmly upon arrival and given a piece of cardboard-like paper and marker.

Ministers: *the leader, three lectors, two voices, musicians, and leader of song (lectors and voices will come forward from the assembly)*

Materials: *table, two-foot-long purple ribbons, glass bowl of water and greenery, lectern, scripture, chair, cardboard papers, and markers*

Gathering Rites

CALL TO WORSHIP *(taken from Psalm 42)*[1]

Leader: "As a deer longs for flowing streams,

All: so my soul longs for you, O God.

Leader: My soul thirsts for God, for the living God.

All: When shall I come and behold the face of God?

Leader: My tears have been my food day and night,

All: while people say to me continually, 'Where is your God?'

Leader: These things I remember, as I pour out my soul:

All: how I went with the throng,

and led them in procession to the house of God,

Leader: with glad shouts and songs of thanksgiving,

All: a multitude keeping festival."

OPENING HYMN

"Come to the Feast," text by Marty Haugen, based on Isaiah 55, tune by Marty Haugen, © 1991, GIA Publications, Inc.

Liturgy of the Word

FIRST READING: WISDOM 7:1–3, 6–14

PSALM 63

"Your Love Is Finer Than Life," text by Marty Haugen, based on Psalm 63, tune by Marty Haugen, © 1982, GIA Publications, Inc.

"Stay with us."

SECOND READING: ACTS 16:6, 9–15, 40

GOSPEL ACCLAMATION

From the "Mass of Creation," text and tune by Marty Haugen, © 1984, GIA Publications, Inc.

REFLECTION

Voice 1:   It all began in the power of the Holy Spirit,
            "forbidding" Paul and Silas to speak God's word in
            Asia,
            driving them westward, across a sea,
            urging them to follow a dream—
            they knew not where or what—
            blowing them across a sea of blue,
            peaceful . . . or perhaps turbulent?

            Yes, they were driven from a placid shore of blue
            by the red-hot love of God,
            poured out like blood . . .
            the transforming libation of new wine.
            And on that first Sabbath, in their first European city,
            by the river, outside the city gates,
            at a synagogue,[2] where women had gathered to pray,
            Paul and Silas encountered transformation
            in a woman, "a dealer in purple cloth."

Voice 2:   Her name was Lydia, we are told . . .
            the name of the region that gave her birth, actually.
            Lydia, back on the other side of the sea,
            that encompassed her hometown of Thyatira,
            was well known for purple dye and the making of
            woolen cloth.

            Lydia . . . a name associated with slavery,
            for slaves were often named
            after their region of origin, once they were freed.
            Lydia . . . a name associated with the smelly,
            perspiring work of dyeing wool,
            dye from the root of a plant, mixed with urine.

Lydia . . . a woman despised because of this
by the "noble" upper class;
but her nobility took another form,
not of socioeconomic status
but of class, as in courage.

Lydia . . . a woman clothed in the purple of courage,
the red of her passionately open-hearted listening
stirred into the blue of Wisdom's seeking her out . . .
crying out by the city gates,
offering her life in abundance,
a feast for all who hunger and thirst.

Lydia . . . moved by and with
the power of the Holy Spirit,
wherever she found it . . .
was a Gentile God-seeker in a Jewish community,
a listener to Spirit-words,
introducing her to Jesus, the Christ.

Voice 1: And she, head of her household—
of coworkers, perhaps, and relatives too?—
was baptized into Christ,
the one who wipes away all distinctions
of Jew or Greek, slave or free, male and female.[3]

She, powerful person of presence,
prevailed then upon Paul . . . urged him
to "come and stay" at her home,
just like those two disciples on the road to Emmaus,
who convinced Jesus to do the same.

She, faithful one, knew what she was doing.
She knew how dangerous it was
to become the presence of Christ
in solidarity with his followers, a speck,
a tiny minority in the Roman colony of Philippi.

Yes, purple became her, revealed her courage.
For not long after Paul and Silas left her home,
the two were arrested, beaten, and imprisoned.
But she would never betray . . . or deny . . .
the truth overflowing her Spirit-filled heart.

"Stay with us."

Indeed, her household became a house church,
beloved of Paul, recipients of his message of joy,
"I thank my God every time I remember you."[4]
And it all began in the power of the Holy Spirit.

MUSICAL REFLECTION
. . . .

"Restless Is the Heart," text and tune by Bernadette Farrell,
© 1989 Bernadette Farrell. Published by OCP Publications.

Ritual of Seeking the Face of God
. . . .

Leader: Of this much we can be sure. God is after us . . . calling
and inviting, nudging and thirsting for us, awaiting our
seeking after God in return. Yes, indeed. The God of
the Exodus freed a nation of slaves that they might
become God's "treasured possession."[5] The God of
the Exile spoke "tenderly to Jerusalem"[6]: "Come to
me; listen, so that you may live."[7] The God of
Wisdom promised: only the yoke of her instruction
would provide the rest, joy, and strength of human
longing.[8] Indeed, such a yoke would clothe all who followed Wisdom with the mantle of royalty and priesthood. And in Jesus, the human face of God, we saw
the fulfillment of all God's promises. For Jesus liberat-
ed, consoled, and offered Wisdom's yoke.[9] And Jesus
formed a community of disciples, who were meant to
do the same.

We are that community of disciples . . . seekers of
God's face because God has first sought us out. Today
we honor our "restless hearts" that respond to the living God in our midst. Take a moment of prayerful
reflection now (as "Restless Is the Heart" is played softly)
to name what it is you most desire. What is it you seek
after? Peace? Courage? Giving voice to truth? Integrity?
Compassion? Something else? When you are able,
write down your word on your paper.

Pause

Now, come forward with your word to one of the two people who told Lydia's story of discipleship. (*Each of these two voices will be on either side of the table.*) As you name your word to her, she will clothe you in the purple yoke of royalty and priesthood. Continue around the outside of the worship space until a circle is formed. Then we will walk slowly in a circle, clockwise, lifting our words high, proclaiming in this way our desire for the living God.

MUSIC DURING THE PROCESSIONS:
. . . .

"My Soul Is Thirsting," text by the Confraternity of Christian Doctrine, based on Psalm 63; tune by Michael Joncas, © 1987. GIA Publications, Inc.

or

"God, Beyond All Names," text and tune by Bernadette Farrell, © 1990, Bernadette Farrell. Published by OCP Publications.

Closing Rites
. . . .

BLESSING
. . . .

Leader:	Seekers after God, all, may we encounter our heart's desire.
All:	Amen!
Leader:	Lovers of God, all, may we savor our beloved.
All:	Amen!
Leader:	Disciples of Jesus, all, may we wear his yoke of prophesy and priesthood for the building of God's kindom.
All:	Amen! Yes! Let it be!

"Stay with us."

CLOSING HYMN

• • • • • • • • • • • •

"As a Fire Is Meant for Burning," text by Ruth Duck, © 1992, GIA Publications, Inc.; tune is Beach Spring, harm. by Marty Haugen, © 1985, GIA Publications, Inc.

Lydia

• •

It's no wonder that infants love to play "peek a boo," and that children delight in the game of hide and seek. The one who wasn't there, suddenly appears! Indeed, was there all along, just in hiding. Isn't it symbolic of the human search for God, initiated by the tenderly persistent, insistent yearning of God for every human heart? I'm reminded of the lover in the Song of Songs (3:1–2): "Upon my bed at night I sought him whom my soul loves; I sought him, but found him not; I called him, but he gave no answer. 'I will rise now and go about the city, in the streets and in the squares; I will seek him whom my soul loves.'" Or, these words attributed to Solomon from the Book of Wisdom (7:7, 8:2): "Therefore I prayed, and understanding was given me; I called on God, and the spirit of wisdom came to me. . . . I loved her and sought her from my youth; I desired to take her for my bride, and became enamored of her beauty." The God beyond all names and images is *the* unconditional lover of us all, each and every one of us. And our lives are meant to become that divine/human dance of seeking and finding.

Lydia was engaged with all her being in that dance of life. This essay will briefly explore Lydia's version of the divine/human story of hide and seek.

● ● ● ● ● ● ● ● ● ● ● ● ● ● ●

Precious little is said about "Lydia" in scripture, a scant six verses in the Acts of the Apostles, two of which set the stage for her encounter with Paul.[10] Here's what we know. She is Paul's first European convert, for they encounter one another after he crosses the Aegean Sea to what is now European territory. The conversion takes place in Philippi, "a leading city of the district of Macedonia and a Roman colony,"[11] on a major overland route from Asia to the West. As was his custom, Paul proceeds to a "place of prayer" on the Sabbath day and assumes the position of teacher.[12] What is unusual, however, is that this worshiping community is made up of women. And Lydia, "a worshiper of God" from the city of Thyatira (in the region of Lydia, in present-day western Turkey), and "a dealer in purple cloth,"[13] is among the community. She is so profoundly moved by Paul's words that she is baptized, along with her entire household. Then, with single-mindedness of heart, she prevails upon Paul . . . if he has judged her "to be faithful to the Lord" . . . to "come and stay" at her home.[14] He does so, along with Silas, his traveling companion.

Surely, Lydia knows well the danger of being in solidarity with followers of Jesus. As if to drive home that point, we learn that Paul and Silas find trouble, not long after leaving Lydia's home. They encounter a slave girl and Paul drives a "spirit of divination" out of her "in the name of Jesus Christ."[15] Her owners, who have made considerable money through her utterances, haul them in front of the magistrates. And the magistrates, encouraged by a surly crowd, order the beating, stripping, and jailing of Paul and Silas. But God intervenes. The two missionaries are set free . . . and even convert the jailer in the process. They return to Lydia's home, where they encourage "the brothers and sisters there" before they depart.[16] Clearly, Lydia's home is a house church, "the cradle of the Christian community in Philippi,"[17] much loved by Paul. This is Paul's story . . . and Lydia's story . . . both intense lovers of God. But, above all, it is God's story, danced in and through Paul and Lydia. For it is God who takes pains to set Paul on his westward course, calling to him in a dream.[18] And it is God who opens the heart of Lydia "to listen eagerly to what was said by Paul."[19]

Until recently, it has been agreed that Lydia was a well-to-do leader of her house church. But newer research, especially on the society

"Stay with us."

and culture of the day, has opened up some other possibilities. Indeed, Ivoni Richter Reimer and Luise Schottroff make a strong case that she was among the lower class, a hard working woman in a "smelly" trade.[20] While her product was certainly appreciated, her profession was not. Plutarch says this: "Often we take pleasure in a thing, but we despise the one who made it. Thus we value aromatic salves and purple clothing, but the dyers and salve-makers remain for us common and low craftspersons."[21] Urine was necessary for dyeing; and dye houses were kept outside cities for that very reason. They were smelly places of business, just like tanneries . . . usually run by women, along with slaves and freed persons.[22] Even Lydia's name points to her low socioeconomic status. For she does not have a "proper name." That is, she is not identified either by her hometown (e.g. Mary of Magdala or Martha of Bethany), or by her relationship to a man (e.g. "Mary, the mother of John whose other name was Mark" of Acts 12:12). Like many a freed slave, she is named only by her region of origin, Lydia.

While few words are said about Lydia, those words are generating more and more questions. We know she wholeheartedly seeks after God, but what is this "place of prayer" in which Paul first encounters her? And who comprises her household? What is the significance of her household in her day? And in ours?

A "WORSHIPER OF GOD"

The God-seeker Lydia is literally named a "worshiper of God." Often this phrase is translated as "God-fearer," which has a very specific meaning. Most scholars, following the classic work of K.G. Kuhn, agree that Lydia is a Gentile "who attended synagogue worship, believed in Jewish monotheism, and kept some part of the ceremonial law, but who did not take the step of full conversion to Judaism."[23]

But the real question is: what is this "place of prayer," this gathering of women where Paul and Lydia encounter one another? Is it a synagogue? Simply a gathering of women out in the open? A gathering of women inside a building? Clearly there is cultic practice going on here. For the Greek word, meaning to "gather" or "assemble," is used by Luke only "in connection with *discipleship and shared work*," as in missionary work.[24] And typically, as the

---

Jewish historian Emil Schurer notes, synagogues were often built by a river or other body of water, so that everyone "could perform the necessary ablutions before taking part in worship."[25] Indeed, Philo of Alexandria (writing in the mid-second century) uses the Greek words for "place of prayer" and "synagogue" interchangeably, as does Josephus to a lesser degree.[26] Those who claim that this gathering of women cannot be a synagogue say this: there were too few Jews in Philippi to form a synagogue, the Greek word for synagogue is not used, and only women were present.[27] The real issue seems to revolve around the last point. Because there are no men, most commentators conclude that it is not a "proper" Jewish worship service. But David Lertis Matson and Richter Reimer disagree. And their disagreement is based largely upon Paul's custom of preaching and teaching in the synagogue on the Sabbath.[28] For Matson, Lydia is meeting with women "in a synagogue of the Jews, albeit a highly irregular one."[29] Furthermore, he believes, Luke deliberately uses the Greek word for "place of prayer" in order to heighten the importance of Lydia's conversion.[30] Indeed, her conversion extends the meaning of the Council of Jerusalem, concluded just prior to Paul's adventure into Philippi. Whereas that Council had opened up Christianity to Gentile men (by concluding that they did not need to be circumcised), Lydia's conversion opens up Christianity for Gentile women.[31] It is a woman's household that becomes the first Gentile base for Paul. This, indeed, is the work of God's Spirit, not unlike the Council of Jerusalem.

HER HOUSEHOLD?
. . . .

Lydia's conversion is one of four household conversion stories in the Acts of the Apostles, and hers is the only one headed by a woman.[32] We are not told who makes up her household. Is she a widow, with or without children? Is it a working household, comprised of relatives and slaves and/or freed slaves? We don't know. But it is a Christian center not unlike that of Simon, the tanner (Acts 9:43, 10:6).

Lydia's story takes place during Paul's inaugural mission into European territory; his evangelizing will now replace that of Peter. And Paul's missionary companion is Silas, one of two bearers of a Spirit-filled letter from the Council of Jerusalem. The Good News is that Gentile men are readily invited into the Christian community without hardship.[33] As has already been noted, Lydia

"Stay with us."

wholeheartedly responds to Paul's preaching, urging him to "come and stay" at her home. Such "staying" implies a communal meal, as in the meal at the home of the two disciples on the road to Emmaus. Such "staying," therefore, further implies the presence of Christ at this meal. By the end of the story, her household has replaced the Jewish "place of prayer." It has become the house church at Philippi, beloved of Paul.

HER SIGNIFICANCE FOR TODAY

For all that we don't know about Lydia, we do know this: She is a courageous seeker after God. She is one of the few women in the Acts of the Apostles who actually speaks. She has power, in both leadership and presence. And that power comes from the depths of her faith. She understands the danger of inviting Paul and Silas into her household, but she cannot do otherwise. She knows she might endanger her business, on which she depends for subsistence, and maybe even her life. But she risks everything to join in solidarity with them, to form a living cell, a mustard seed of faith, an alternative community to the dominating Roman culture that literally surrounds her story. What might she say to those of us who envision Church as a living organism, an alternative gospel vision in the midst of a dominating Roman culture?

SOME RESOURCES

Abrahamsen, Valerie. "Women at Philippi: The Pagan and Christian Evidence." *Journal of Feminist Studies in Religion* 3, no. 2 (Fall 1987): 17–30.

Hollyday, Joyce. "Lydia: A Hunger for the Gospel," in *Clothed With the Sun: Biblical Women, Social Justice, and Us.* Louisville, Kentucky: Westminster John Knox Press, 1994, 183–85.

Matson, David Lertis. "The Household Conversions of Lydia [Acts 16:11–15], The Roman Jailer [Acts 16:25–34], and Crispus [Acts 18:1–11]," in *Household Conversion Narratives in Acts: Pattern and Interpretation.* Sheffield: Sheffield Academic Press, 1996, 35–83.

O'Day, Gail. "Acts," in *Women's Bible Commentary, Expanded Edition With Apocrypha,* edited by Carol A. Newsom and Sharon H. Ringe. Louisville, Kentucky: Westminster John Knox Press, 1998, 394–402.

Portefaix, Lilian. *Sisters Rejoice: Paul's Letter to the Philippians and Luke-Acts as Seen by First-Century Philippian Women. Coniectanae Biblica* New Testament Series 20. Stockholm: Almquist & Wiksell International, 1988.

Richter Reimer, Ivoni. "Lydia and Her House (16:13–15, 40)," in *Women in the Acts of the Apostles: A Feminist Liberation Perspective*. Translated by Linda M. Maloney. Minneapolis: Fortress Press, 1995, 71–149.

Schottroff, Luise. "Lydia: A New Quality of Power," in *Let the Oppressed Go Free: Feminist Perspectives on the New Testament*. Translated by Annemarie S. Kidder. Louisville, Ky.: Westminster John Knox Press, 1993, 131–137.

Sleevi, Mary Lou. "Lydia," in *Women of the Word*. Notre Dame: Ave Maria Press, 1989, 92–96.

NOTES

• • • • •

1. See Psalm 42:1–4.

2. There has been much discussion around "the place of prayer," as the Greek literally says. Is it a synagogue? A gathering within a house of worship? Or, a gathering outdoors, by the river? (It is known that Jews typically gathered for prayer by a river to provide water for the necessary ablutions.) Those who believe that this gathering is not a synagogue claim that there were not many Jews in Philippi (probably not true), that the word synagogue is not used, and that it is a group of women who are praying. For this latter reason alone, a number of commentators claim that it is not, in any case, a "proper" Jewish worship service. And yet Philo and Josephus use the Greek word meaning "place of prayer" interchangeably with the word synagogue. For more on this, see Ivoni Richter Reimer, *Women in the Acts of the Apostles*, trans. by Linda M. Maloney (Minneapolis: Fortress Press, 1995), 82–86.

3. See Galatians 3:28.

4. Philippians 1:3.

5. See Exodus 19:5.

6. See Isaiah 40:2.

7. See Isaiah 55:3.

8. See Sirach 6:23–31, 51:26.

9. See Matthew 11:28–30.

10. Acts 16:11–15, 40.

11. Acts 16:12.

12. According to Ivoni Richter Reimer, in her *Women in the Acts of the Apostles* trans. by Linda M. Maloney (Minneapolis: Fortress Press, 1995), 75, the two Greek words which translate into "sit down to speak" are found whenever Jesus sat down to teach. Furthermore, she notes on page 77 that "whenever it is a question of religious praxis or matters related to faith, and whenever the location is a cultic place," the use of these verbs "indicates that what happens here is teaching, interpretation and preaching of the scriptures."

13. Acts 16:14.

14. Acts 16:15. Her urging of Paul, and her prevailing upon him, are reminiscent of the two disciples on the road to Emmaus, who urge Jesus to come into their home at the end of the day, as they arrive in Emmaus (Luke 24:29). These are the only two stories in the New Testament where that common word is used.

15. Acts 16:16, 16:18.

16. Acts 16:40.

17. S. Heine, *Women and Early Christianity*, trans. by John Bowden (London: SCM Press, 1987), 84, as found in David Lertis Matson, *Household Conversion Narratives in Acts: Pattern and Interpretation* (Sheffield. England: Sheffield Academic Press, 1996), 148.

18. See Acts 16:6–10.

19. Acts 16:14.

20. See Richter Reimer, pp. 71–130. And also see Luise Schottroff, "Lydia: A New Quality of Power," in *Let the Oppressed Go Free: Feminist Perspectives on the New Testament*, trans. by Annemarie S. Kidder (Louisville, Ky.: Westminster/John Knox Press, 1993), pp. 131–37. Schottroff's article will hereafter be noted as Schottroff.

21. Richter Reimer, p. 107.

22. Schottroff, p. 132.

23. Richter Reimer, p. 93. Of course, this full conversion of which K.G. Kuhn spoke is symbolized by circumcision, which only applies to males.

24. Richter Reimer, p. 73.

25. Emil Schurer, *The History of the Jewish People in the Age of Jesus Christ*, pp. 440–41, as found in Matson, footnote #54, p. 145.

26. Richter Reimer, p. 85–86.

27. Richter Reimer, pp. 82–83.

28. Richter Reimer also points to considerable evidence of inscriptions in the Mediterranean world of this time to conclude that the two words are used interchangeably; see pp. 87–90.

29. Matson, p. 146.

30. It is important to remember that every one of Jesus' significant life events took place in prayer, according to Luke.

31. Matson, p. 152.

32. The others are Cornelius (Acts 10:1–33), the Roman jailer (16:25–34), and Crispus (18:5–8).

33. See Acts 15:22–35.

five

Eᴠᴇ

We Are Formed in Wisdom

··

As Told by Eve's Daughter

··

In this form of Morning Prayer, we celebrate God's birthing us, male and female, into the divine image, into Wisdom. And yet, we remain sinful, in continual need of God's birthing us into the fullness of life. The tree of life symbolizes this birthing; as such, it is central to the space. There is also space for musicians and a place for the leader, readers, and storyteller.

Ministers: *prayer leader, two readers, the Daughter of Eve as story-teller, the musicians, and cantor*

Materials: *Tree of Life (The composition of the tree is open to the imagination of the planners. However, it might consist of a large wooden cross, adorned with flowers or greenery.)*

Gathering Rites

CALL TO WORSHIP

Leader: In the beginning, the breath of God whooshed over the formless waters.

All: Yes, "She Who Is . . . sheer aliveness,"[1] expansive, unending Being . . . contracted in labor . . .

Leader: and birthed the light of day and darkness of night . . . the sky, earth, and seas . . . vegetation . . . sun, moon, and stars . . . and creatures of the sea and earth.

All: But love could not contain herself, and she made room for more . . . for two, each in the divine image.

Leader: Tired, but deeply satisfied, she rested . . . for a moment . . . but not before she had pronounced her work "very good" indeed!

All: She Who Is . . . irrepressible, generating, quickening, liberating, life-giving . . . chooses to create . . . again and again . . . in, with, and through us, on our pilgrim path of life.

OPENING HYMN

"Come, Sophia," text by Miriam Therese Winter, © 1995, Medical Mission Sisters. Tune is NETTLETON ("Sing a New Church" is a contemporary hymn to that same tune) from J. Wyeth's *Repository of Sacred Music, Pt. II*, 1813.

Come, Sophia, Holy Wisdom, gateway to eternity.
Sacred Source of all that is from long before earth came to be,
In your womb the primal waters from below and from above,
gently rock Your sons and daughters, born to wisdom and to love.

Come, Sophia, be a clear compelling presence everywhere.
Still the terror, dry the tears; come, ease the burdens that we bear.

"Then their eyes were opened."

From the first faint light of morning, through the dark when
　　day is done,
be the midwife of our borning and the rising of our sun.

Come, Sophia, intuition weaving wisdom deep within,
bringing promise to fruition through the prophets that have
been,
pleading justice for tomorrow and forgiveness for today
for the images we borrow and the roles we often play.

Come, Sophia, we believe You are the shaman of the soul.
Break us open to receive You; fill us up and make us whole.
You inspire us to envision all the fullness of shalom
on a new path through tradition that will surely lead us home.

OPENING PRAYER
. . . .

All:　　　　Laboring, birthing, creating God,
　　　　　　In the beginning, Your boundless love
　　　　　　energized chaos into order . . . delight . . . Eden . . .
　　　　　　man and woman.
　　　　　　In every beginning, Intimate One,
　　　　　　You breathe Your Spirit of Justice, Mercy, and
　　　　　　Forgiveness
　　　　　　into human flesh, made in your image,
　　　　　　that our eyes may be opened to your Wisdom,
　　　　　　both now and forevermore. Amen.

Liturgy of the Word
. . . .

PSALM 63
. . . .

"In the Shadow of Your Wings," text by David Haas, based on
Psalm 63, tune by David Haas, © 1986, GIA Publications, Inc.

READING: ISAIAH (42:5, 14–16)
. . . .

Voice 1:　　Thus says God, the Lord,
　　　　　　who created the heavens and stretched them out,
　　　　　　who spread out the earth and what comes from it,

"Then their eyes were opened."

who gives breath to the people upon it
and spirit to those who walk in it.

Voice 2:   For a long time I have held my peace,
I have kept still and restrained myself;
now I will cry out like a woman in labor,
I will gasp and pant.
I will lay waste mountains and hills,
and dry up all their herbage;
I will turn the rivers into islands, and dry up the pools.
I will lead the blind by a road they do not know,
by paths they have not known I will guide them.
I will turn the darkness before them into light,
the rough places into level ground.
These are the things I will do, and I will not forsake
them.

PSALM 16

· · · · · · · ·

"You Will Show Me the Path of Life," Refrain 1, text by Marty
Haugen, based on Psalm 16:1–2, 6–10; tune by Marty Haugen, ©
1988, GIA Publications, Inc.

REFLECTION BY THE DAUGHTER OF EVE

· ·

"Tell me how it was in the beginning," I would say. And my mama,
Eve, would put all her work aside and tell me the story I loved to
hear, one more time.

Mama was older when she gave birth to us, my sisters and brothers
and me.[2] She was no longer brand new, "dripping wet," fresh "from
God's fingers."[3] But, without fail, every time she began the story,
there was a catch in her voice . . . and a youthful radiance on her
face . . . at the wonder of it all. And without fail, I would glimpse
the indelible mark of God, impressed on her forever. She would
begin with a small smile and a faraway look in her eye. Then a little
laugh, as she remembered the monkeys chattering away in the garden, mimicking Adam and her. I could see it all! Sparkling, gurgling
rivers. Luscious fruit. And vivid flowers, splashed like so many colors across an artist's palette. She and Papa had everything they
needed. They were protected . . . innocent . . . like children at play.

"Then their eyes were opened."

Then came the day when *everything* changed. Mama said she'd begun to notice things. That they were like God, she and Papa. Curious. Intelligent. Creative. And responsible. For God had told them that *they* were to care for all this creation. But how? It seemed to Mama that they needed so much more wisdom for that kind of responsibility. Should they eat the fruit of the tree of knowledge of good and evil? Or not? They made their choice, freely, both of them. And as Mama put it, their eyes "were opened, and they knew that they were naked."[4] Yes, that was the difference. Now they *knew* that they were vulnerable. Limited. Groping for answers. Stripped bare of all disguise. Exposed to harm. Evil. Death. And destruction. Now they *knew* the harm they could do. And the goodness, as well. They were creature, not Creator. But the divine imprint remained . . . never to be totally rubbed out. No, their divine vulnerability could produce intimacy, community, forgiveness, love— to the point of giving life for another. The choice would now be theirs, again and again and again.

Indeed, they had already chosen. And there would be consequences. For God sent them on the path of *their* choice. The pilgrim path of wisdom. Of becoming fully human. This much they knew. Wisdom would be a long time in coming. But they would *not* be abandoned. For love tenderly clothed them in the garments they would need along the way.

MUSIC
· · · · ·

Refrain I only of Psalm 16, "You Will Show Me the Path of Life," sung twice.

Mama has learned so much by now. And she hands it on to me . . . and to my brothers and sisters. She learned, first of all, how connected she was to everything and everyone . . . in all creation. To Adam, of course, but it was different than before. Because she began to learn how very much they could hurt each other. He blamed her! And she lashed back at him! It took them both time . . . alone . . . hurting . . . until they could come back together. That was their first forgiveness, and she knew that God was very pleased.[5] Then there was her connection to the serpent. Oh, not as you might think, in matters of deceit. No, it was that her skin could not contain her. She had to keep shedding what she had become in order to grow. At this point, her eyes would get a dreamy look. Her voice would become hushed. And I would hear, one more time, the tale of that sacred morning. Early, at dawn, when the dew was still glistening on the grass. Suddenly, in her very gut, her body remembered. She and the earth were one. Love itself had tenderly shaped her from the kindred earth.

Yes, Wisdom took root in Mama, little by little, as she continued to risk . . . to struggle . . . to persevere . . . and choose life, again and again. There were the easy times, the times of pure joy—a glance of profound love . . . a hand held in wordless understanding . . . a sunset streaked with the fingerprints of God. At those times, she said, she could almost hear the song that gave her birth.[6] And there were the creative times—with every quickening . . . every impulse to give birth . . . every contraction of hard labor . . . every satisfying release of new life. Whether a daughter or a son . . . or the work of human hands. But, Wisdom came even in the emptiness, in the seeming absence of God . . . in the silence that can divide and separate. When Mama took the time to listen . . . she became aware of a gnawing for something or someone . . . beyond, just over the horizon. And she came to know well the temptation that went along with it. To settle for less . . . to get hooked on a cheap substitute for the God who *is* the beyond. But, the more she resisted this temptation, the more she discovered the greatest gift of all. God, the beyond, was within, closer than an evening stroll in the garden. *This* is what it meant to her to be made in the image of God.

And finally, Mama would always end the story like this. "Remember the Tree of Life," she would say. "It's still beyond our reach, but it's *so* important. Someday, I don't know how, I don't know when, that tree will fulfill God's promises." And then she would describe this tree, stroking it with her very words. It was as though she had memorized every knothole, every scar, every leaf, every sign of life. "Remember the Tree of Life."

I am daughter of Eve. Woman, created in the image of God. Formed in the image of Wisdom. Pilgrim on the path of life. Mother of the living.

. . . .

"Tree of Life," text by Marty Haugen, tune is THOMAS adapted by Marty Haugen, © 1984, GIA Publications, Inc.

Ritual of Reverencing the Tree of Life
. . . .

INVITATION BY THE LEADER
. . . .

In the beginning, God birthed a universe, and it was "good." But God was not done yet. For divine love could not be contained. It poured forth into two, male and female, made in the divine image, blessed with authority to continue the process of creation. And God saw that it was "very good." In time, humanity used, misused, and abused this power. But God was not done yet, for God continued to create, to birth a people through the prophets. And then, in the fullness of time, the Wisdom of God loved us enough to birth a Son, the one who would enflesh this love. Fully. But for some, he was too much. And he was nailed to a tree. In that ultimate act of love, he stretched out his arms wide before breathing his last, so that the tree itself became the birthing instrument of life eternal.

What does it take for *us* to follow the pilgrim path of life? To birth a new creation, again and again, in partnership with God? Nothing less than this. Love that cannot be contained. God's kind of love. A love that seeds . . . and forms a nurturing space for growth. A love that gives and receives, that is willing to risk, to enter into the unknown. That is willing to confront fear. Is it dangerous? Will it hurt? Will the change be too much? A love that is mature. That is willing to live with ambiguity and paradox. That is willing to put another's good before one's own. A love that simply rejoices in the good and learns to let go, allowing the new life to create a destiny of its own.

The tree of life is symbolic of that kind of love. Before we come forward to reverence this tree in whatever way we wish, we pray for all those people and places in our creation that are still groaning, longing to see Wisdom's love.

"Then their eyes were opened."

INTERCESSIONS

Please respond "O Holy Wisdom, birth us anew." *Each community creates its own petitions out of its own needs and the needs of the church and the world.*

The Ritual of Reverencing the Tree of Life

The leader calls everyone forward, while the musicians play and sing the following . . . and any other appropriate hymns.

MUSIC DURING THE RITUAL

"God, Beyond All Names," text and tune by Bernadette Farrell, © 1990, Bernadette Farrell. Published by OCP Publications.

THE LORD'S PRAYER *(sung if possible)*

Closing Rites

FINAL BLESSING

The leader invites everyone to extend an arm of blessing on the assembly and respond "Amen" to the following.

Leader: May we walk the pilgrim path of life, with Holy Wisdom at our side.

All: Amen!

Leader: May we be filled to overflowing with love and courage, enough to birth God's creation, again and again.

All: Amen!

Leader: May we continue to have our eyes opened to Wisdom, for the sake of every new world.

All: Amen!

"Then their eyes were opened."

"Simple Gifts," eighteenth-century Shaker hymn.

Some Thoughts on Eve
. . . .

How did we get here? What was it like in the beginning? Why do we suffer? And even die . . . when we *know* that God is good? What does it mean to be human? Eternal questions. Our questions. And those of our ancestors in faith. Once the Israelites knew themselves to be God's people, these questions became paramount. For God had heard their cries of anguish in Egypt and answered their pleas for deliverance. Yes, their eagle-winged God had created them into a people, a "treasured possession . . . a priestly kingdom and a holy nation."[7] So it was that a story emerged from the questions, a story of Adam and Eve, a story of beginnings.

Eve is central to this story. And she comes to us today with plenty of baggage. Eve, the "sinner." Responsible for the sin of the world. Responsible for "the fall." Where does all this baggage come from? Consider this: The sage, "Jesus son of Eleazar son of Sirach of Jerusalem" (Ecclesiasticus or Sirach 50:27), is the first to say to us, "From a woman sin had its beginning, and because of her we all die" (Sir 25:24).[8] Gradually, this view takes hold. The writer of the First Letter to Timothy tells us, "For Adam was formed first, then Eve; and Adam was not deceived, but the woman was deceived and became a transgressor" (2:13–14). Such attitudes toward Eve become increasingly common in religious literature. Furthermore, Eve becomes associated more and more with sexuality and lust, "with the serpent playing an increasingly satanic and phallic role. And of course the more Eve is identified as the source of sin, the more urgent becomes the need to control, subdue and dominate her."[9] She becomes every woman, source of sin, even though sin is never mentioned in the biblical story of Eve.[10] Neither is the "fall," though the powerful brush of John Milton's poetry in

"*Then their eyes were opened.*"

Paradise Lost has imprinted that image on our minds and hearts to this very day.

How is it possible to hear the story of Eve with fresh ears, without the commentaries we have taken in as part and parcel of the story? Feminist scholars, committed to the God of liberating life, have begun to be suspicious about interpretations that demean and destroy life and to ask new questions of the text. Phyllis Trible was among the first to offer us some new perspectives on Eve.[11] She clearly shows that God intends to establish equal human partners—male and female made in the divine image—who are responsible for the earth and all living creatures (see Genesis 1:27). Even in the second story of creation (Gn 2:4–3:24), the "earth creature" (namely, Adam) is not yet sexually differentiated at the beginning of the story. It is only after God places Adam in a deep sleep and brings forth the woman from his side that Adam rejoices (in Gn 2:23a), "This at last is bone of my bones and flesh of my flesh!" It is only then that the earth creature renames himself 'ish (man), partner to 'ishshah (woman), reflecting God's intent that the earth creature will have "a helper as his partner" (Gn 2:18)[12] or "a suitable counterpart."[13]

But it is the feminist scripture scholar Carol Meyers who develops the thesis that Eve represents Everywoman at the time of premonarchic rural Israel. For Meyers, the second creation story reflects the experience, questions, and wisdom of a people who lived a thousand years before Christ in the "hill country," along the spine of Palestine. Life there was hard, and water was scarce. It was gathered up from the winter rains, like precious drops of dew, into deep cisterns that had been carved out of the bedrock that lay close to the surface of the hilltops. And the land yielded its fruit grudgingly, only after long hours of human toil. Onto this scene steps Everywoman. She lives within a peasant household. There are several possible configurations of such households, based on extended and/or multiple families. She has certain responsibilities that are hers alone, especially the bearing and raising of children and the preparation of food. Men have other responsibilities, especially the back-breaking labor of farming and defense of the land. But, in that "pioneer" time, she often shares some responsibilities with the men, such as craft production and the education of her children. Perhaps, on occasion, she is even involved in the farming. She and her neighbors begin to ask questions like, "If

"Then their eyes were opened."

God is a God of blessing, how did this come to be? How was it in the beginning? How do we find meaning and wisdom in all the paradoxes of life?" Thus it was, according to Meyers, that the second creation story developed. Notice the references in Gn 3:17–19 to the difficult farming life that the peasants certainly experienced. Notice, too, the idyllic picture of lush greenness painted at the beginning of this second creation account that might well have come out of a yearning for enough water. It is a myth, a story of human meaning. It is an etiology, a way of explaining how things came to be as they are. And it is a wisdom tale that developed out of human experience.

And yet, old notions of Eve stubbornly persist, partly because of translation, partly because of worldview. Both Meyers and Rabbi Elyse Goldstein, another feminist scripture scholar, tackle the task of translation, begun earlier by Phyllis Trible. Both of them scrutinize the difficult passage, Gn 3:16, which has contributed to the notion of male superiority. The NRSV translation reads this way, "To the woman he said, 'I will greatly increase your pangs in childbearing; in pain you shall bring forth children, yet your desire shall be for your husband, and he shall rule over you.'" According to Meyers, the Hebrew word for increase is *rbh*, which is usually used with a particular quantity. It does not make sense to use this word with pain, she notes, as though one could quantify pain. Furthermore, the Hebrew word that is translated as childbearing, *heron*, actually means pregnancy. Thus, she would translate the first part of this verse, "I will greatly increase your toil and your pregnancies. Along with travail shall you beget children."[14] But there is still that troublesome statement of male rule at the conclusion of this verse. Here Rabbi Goldstein offers us something. She points out that the Hebrew word for rule has another meaning, one that is primary, in fact. It means to serve as a model or example. Her translation, then, of the second part of the verse is this: "Your desire shall be for your husband, and he shall model himself after you."[15] She concludes that the woman is a role model of "fidelity and sexual stability."[16] And like numerous other scripture scholars, she insists that God's *intent* is to create male/female equality.

What about worldview? Theology—faith seeking understanding, God talk—always takes place within a context of time, place, and worldview. For the ancients, the earth was the center of the universe. God and heaven were "up," evil spirits were "down below," and creation was perfect until humans "messed things up." And serpents were the voice of temptation, symbolic of deities— including goddesses— in opposition to Yahweh, the living God of Israel. But today we know differently. We are *not* the center of the universe. Not only that, the universe, begun over fifteen billion years ago, is continually expanding. By contrast, reflective human life on earth is perhaps only thirty thousand years old. What can we say, then, about the story of Eve, from the perspective of *our* worldview? For us who believe, God is *still* an abundantly loving Creator, humans are *still* made in God's image, male and female, and God's intent is *still* equal partnership between the sexes. God *still* desires an intimate relationship with us, all the while remaining Mystery, beyond human understanding. And humans *still* bear responsibility for their choices, while sin still causes human diminishment and domination/subordination. But, what if the first humans were imperfect from the beginning, *always* in need of wisdom? What if the human condition has *always* been about movement on the pathway of life?

How, then, might Eve emerge from *our* questions? How can we put on new glasses as we take another look at Eve? Let me share with you a delightful surprise on a recent trip to a bookstore. My train of thought went something like this, "Why, it's a book about Eve! In the children's department! Hmmm. The pictures are wonderful . . . I think I'll get it for myself . . . and for my granddaughter." This creative little book, *The Blessing Seed: A Creation Myth for the New Millennium*, just might provide the lens we need to take a fresh look at Eve, a much-maligned woman.[17] In this book, Eve is a seeker after wisdom, a woman who is much loved by God. She has eaten the fruit before it is ripe because she is so eager to discover God's special gift to humans. God explains to her and Adam that they will need to travel the four paths of wisdom in order to discover their special gift of learning and caring. "The four paths are called the path of wonder, the path of emptiness, the path of making, and the path of coming home."[18] God then gently describes each of these paths and sends them off with a blessing. It is only then that they are ready to spread the special seeds already inside them; it is only then that they are ready to embark on the archetypal adventure of the human spirit. Is this the Eve we've been waiting for?

"Then their eyes were opened."

SOME RESOURCES
· · · · · · · · · · · · · · · ·

Frankel, Ellen, Ph.D. *The Five Books of Miriam: A Woman's Commentary on the Torah*. San Francisco: Harper, 1998.

Goldstein, Rabbi Elyse. *ReVisions: Seeing Torah Through a Feminist Lens*. Woodstock, Vt.: Jewish Lights Publishing, 1998.

Matthews, Caitlin, with illustrations by Alison Dexter. *The Blessing Seed: A Creation Myth for the New Millennium*. Bristol, England: Barefoot Books, 1998.

Meyers, Carol. *Discovering Eve: Ancient Israelite Women in Context*. New York & Oxford: Oxford University Press, 1988.

Niditch, Susan. "Genesis," in *Women's Bible Commentary, Expanded Edition, With Apocrypha*, edited by Carol A. Newsom and Sharon H. Ringe. Louisville, Ky.: Westminster John Knox Press, 1998.

Trible, Phyllis. "A Love Story Gone Awry," in *God and the Rhetoric of Sexuality*. Philadelphia: Fortress Press, 1978, 72–143.

NOTES
· · · · ·

1. See Elizabeth A. Johnson, *She Who Is: The Mystery of God in Feminist Theological Discourse* (New York: Crossroad, 1992), 243.

2. See Genesis 5:4.

3. Mary Lou Sleevi, *Women of the Word* (Notre Dame, Ind.: Ave Maria Press, 1989), 15.

4. Genesis 3:7a. I am indebted to a companion on the journey, Martha Garrison, for seeing the connection between the words here and the words in Luke 24:31a.

5. This idea comes from a colleague, Roni Antenucci, a member of our storytelling group, "Women of the Well."

6. This idea comes from Caitlin Matthews, *The Blessing Seed* (Bristol, England: Barefoot Books, 1998).

7. See Exodus 19:5, 6.

8. The writer of Sirach was a teacher in Jerusalem who wrote between 200 and 180 B.C.E.

9. Carol Meyers, *Discovering Eve* (New York & Oxford: Oxford University Press, 1988), 75–76.

10. The word "sin" appears for the first time in Genesis 4:7, with the story of Cain and Abel.

11. See Phyllis Trible, "A Love Story Gone Awry," in *God and the Rhetoric of Sexuality* (Philadelphia: Fortress Press, 1978), 72–143.

12. NRSV translation. Earlier translations did not make clear the intent of partnership, which the Hebrew does intend. For example, the RSV had previously translated this as "a helper fit for him."

13. Translation by Carol Meyers. p. 85.

14. Meyers, pp. 105–8.

15. Rabbi Elyse Goldstein, *ReVisions: Seeing Torah Through Feminist Lens* (Woodstock, Vt.: Jewish Lights Publishing, 1998), 57.

16. Ibid.

17. Caitlin Matthews, *The Blessing Seed* (Bristol, England: Barefoot Books, 1998).

18. From Caitlin Matthews' book; there are no page numbers.

"*Then their eyes were opened.*"

ℳaura Clarke,
Dorothy Kazel,
Ita Ford, & Jean Donovan

We Are Blessed and Broken, That We Might Be Shared[1]

....

A Prayer Service to Remember Dorothy Kazel, Jean Donovan, Ita Ford, and Maura Clarke

....

This prayer service is about walking the way of Jesus, who became bread—blessed, broken, and shared—for us. It is about confronting evil and the powers of domination. It is about being with the ones who suffer the most, for the sake of their healing and empowerment. It is about the radical transformation of human life. It is about four women who walked the road to Emmaus with Jesus . . . Sr. Maura Clarke, Sr. Dorothy Kazel, Sr. Ita Ford, and Jean Donovan. And it is about us.

The central focus is the cross . . . wooden, large, and unadorned. For the cross is at the heart of eucharistic life. It is the scandal that can become a stumbling block, the shame that each of us must look in the eye and confront, and the only way to life.

Ministers: *prayer leader, the two lectors, narrator, four voices (the women who are voices will be wearing a large paper cross, each with the name of the woman they are representing— Maura, Dorothy, Ita, and Jean), musicians, and cantor(s)*

Materials: *the cross, large paper crosses*

Gathering Rites

. . . .

CALL TO WORSHIP

. . . .

Leader: We gather in the sign of the Cross +,

All: a stumbling block to some, and a scandal.

Leader: But, to all who believe, it is assuredly

All: the searchlight of truth,

Leader: faithfulness in the face of fear,

All: undying symbol of unrelenting, unconditional love.

OPENING HYMN

. . . .

"Tree of Life," text by Marty Haugen, tune is THOMAS, adapted by Marty Haugen, © 1984, GIA Publications, Inc. *During the hymn, the cross is carried in by the voices and placed in the center of the worship space.*

"And they recognized him."

Liturgy of the Word

GOSPEL: LUKE 8:1–3[2]

A NARRATION

Narrator: They followed Jesus from Galilee. And from Cleveland, Ohio, Westport, Connecticut, the Bay Ridge section of Brooklyn, and Rockaway Beach. They absorbed the good news, each in her own way. And they brought their resources with them . . . pouring them out in abundance. Luke tells us that the women's discipleship brought them all the way to the cross and the empty tomb, where the angels spoke clearly to them. "Remember how he told you, while he was still in Galilee, that the Son of Man must be handed over to sinners, and be crucified, and on the third day rise again."[3] Four women remembered. And their names were Sr. Maura Clarke, Sr. Dorothy Kazel, Sr. Ita Ford, and Jean Donovan.

Maura: Maura is the oldest. The year is 1931, and the place is New York City. On January 13, Irish immigrants John and Mary Clarke delight in their first-born child. They name her Mary Elizabeth, but affectionately call her Maura. (Pause, shift to the past.) A lover of life, she had a sparkle in her eye. And her feet could never resist the Irish jig. Her mother would remember the pretty green suit she wore the day she entered the Maryknoll novitiate. And everyone would remember her generosity. Some would even call it reckless. For "in Nicaragua . . . she was always drawing advances on her monthly allowance (about $15), because as soon as she got it, she gave it away."[4]

Dorothy: "You were just drawn to Dorothy! She was very pretty, blue sparkling eyes . . . high energy. Always joking. . . ."[5] "She seemed so unaware of her beauty."[6] "She'd be the first to jump in the truck and learn how to drive a stick shift, or the first to hop on a

---

motorcycle—just fully open and accepting to all new challenges."[7] Born on June 30, 1939, in Cleveland, Ohio, Dorothy Kazel was "vivacious, fun-loving, and athletic" . . . with "many friends of both sexes."[8] She was popular, president of her high school senior class. Later on, as a high school guidance counselor in Cleveland Heights, Dorothy was "100 percent present to any person she was speaking with. . . . She had a special feeling for people who had been kicked around—the ones that nobody else wants."[9]

Ita: Ita's spirit of adventure surfaced at age three . . . when she wended her way down busy Brooklyn streets to "go to school" like her older brother Billy. Years later, at Marymount Manhattan College, this spirit simply soared. She set out in a cramped Volkswagen "bug" with two of her close friends, Kate Monahan and Ana May. They "ate hamburgers and french fries and laughed all the way across North America and down into Mexico. . . . Ita's 'Peter Pan' shape and size and haircut puzzled the ticket seller at Disneyland, who admitted her as Ana May's son."[10]

Jean: Jean was the youngest. Born on April 10, 1953, she burst into this world at seven months. Independent. Competitive. A go-getter. Jean "enjoyed the limelight at parties, rode noisy motorcycles, was generous with money, visited bars with her friends, and liked nothing better than a good laugh."[11] She "was raised in an atmosphere of financial security, success and conservative politics" . . . and also "a deep sense of compassion and generosity."[12]

Narrator: Each heard the call of God . . . from a distant shore. And each responded, in her own way.

MUSICAL RESPONSE
. . . .

"Lord, When You Came," verses 1–2. Text is *Pescador de Hombres*, by Cesareo Gabarain, trans. by Willard Francis Jabusch, tune by Cesareo Gabarain, © 1979, published by OCP Publications, translation © 1994, GIA Publications, Inc.

"And they recognized him.."

Narrator: A cry pierces the heavens. Birthed ages ago, out of agony. Birthed again and again, like an unfinished symphony of faith, from every corner of the globe. For much of this past century, it howled from El Salvador, land of the Savior. A tiny, "concentrated little bouillon cube of a country."[13] Full of spunky, energetic people.

Lector 1: O Lord, how long shall the wicked,
how long shall the wicked exult?
They pour out their arrogant words;
all the evildoers boast.
They crush your people, O Lord,
and afflict your heritage.
They kill the widow and the stranger,
they murder the orphan,
And they say, "The Lord does not see" (Psalm 94:3–7a).

Narrator: Why, O God, why?
Our people despair.
The heavy hand of the rich and powerful . . .
the "Fourteen Families" . . . weighs us down.
Government coup follows government coup,
but nothing changes . . .
nothing but terror and torture.
Is there no end?

Lector 1: Who rises up for me against the wicked?
Who stands up for me against evildoers? (Psalm 94:16).

MUSICAL RESPONSE
. . . .

"Lord, When You Came," verses 3–4.

Each of the four certain women come forward to claim their call.

Maura: My first Maryknoll assignment was not to a distant shore, though it might as well have been. Right here in the Bronx, so many children were in pain! From hunger . . . beatings at home, and feelings of "no way out". Then, late in 1959, I was off to Siuna, Nicaragua. A small gold mining town, where so many lived in shanties, "infested with mosquitoes, vermin and rats."[14] And the wealthy literally looked down from "on high." As principal of the school there, three years later, I would begin to agonize. Was charity enough? Some of the sisters were demanding so much more: living and working among the poorest of the poor. In the end, I joined them . . . in the barrios outside Managua. It was there that I came to see "the rulers and the military as the high priests" . . . and the poor "as the tortured Jesus."[15] But, my most difficult assignment was a return to the United States, away from my beloved people. Someone had to tell of the horrors of the Samoza regime, Maryknoll said. And I was the one! So it was that I would celebrate—with profound gratitude—the end of the Samoza regime from North American shores. Then, finally, on August 5, 1980, I returned to the people I loved. This time to El Salvador . . . and my new ministry partner, Ita Ford.

Dorothy: My life seemed all set. College. Engagement to a young man from California. That is, until I encountered the Ursuline Sisters. There was something so impressive about them. . . . Was marriage what I really wanted? How I agonized over my decision! In the end, I chose the Ursulines . . . and life with the Cleveland Missionary Team in El Salvador. In 1974, La Libertad was deceptively peaceful. The Pacific breezes of this small fishing town were a reminder of days gone by, when it had been a haven for surfers. But, little by little, waves of government terror began lapping on the shore . . . creating instead a community of people trapped in fear. So, our ministry revolved around the needs of the people. Empowering leaders, *promoción*, we called it. And most of all, teaching people that they had human dignity because they were children of God. What a threat this became to some men in power!

Ita: Missionary work was in my blood. Maryknoll was in my blood. My uncle, Francis X. Ford, had suffered martyrdom in China as a Maryknoll bishop. But this call did not penetrate my heart and soul until a college trip to Eastern Europe and the Soviet Union. The year

"And they recognized him."

was 1961. It was then that I witnessed "soul-wrenching belief."[16] It was then that I saw people "who really deserved freedom of religion."[17] It was then that I knew I had to become a Maryknoll sister. My dream finally became reality, despite an agonizing delay of final vows due to a mysterious illness. In 1973, I was assigned to Chile, to the squatters' neighborhoods outside Santiago. Just in time to witness the overthrow of the Allende regime, with American assistance. Just in time to witness the brutality of the new Pinochet dictatorship. And with my dear friend and colleague, Sr. Carla Piette, I kept asking myself, "Am I willing to suffer with the people here, the suffering of the powerless?"[18] All we wanted to do was to build the reign of God. But five years of terror . . . of killing after killing after killing would leave me seething like a volcano. I desperately needed time off! Then, after a break, Carla and I began our ministry again. This time in the spring of 1980, among the refugees of a brutal, undeclared civil war in Chalatenango, the northern province of El Salvador.

Jean: My path was a most unlikely one, you might say. A degree in accounting from Mary Washington College in 1975. An MBA at Case Western Reserve. A position at Arthur Andersen accounting firm in Cleveland. But, whispers of my junior year in Cork, Ireland, would not leave me alone. It was there that Father Michael Crowley told stories of his ten years in the barrios of Peru. It was there that he challenged me to see differently, to hear differently, to develop "a sense of global consciousness."[19] Nineteen seventy-seven was a big year for me. I met and fell in love with a medical student, Doug Cable. But, I also applied for and was accepted into Cleveland's Missionary Team. On August 10, 1979, I arrived in El Salvador, to work with Dorothy. I was only twenty-six years old, and "Dottie" was much more mature. But she was young at heart and youthful in appearance. We were "a fun-loving pair."[20] And passionate about the people.

Narrator: The paths of these four would intersect in El Salvador in August 1980.

MUSICAL REFLECTION

"In Her Poor," text and tune by Colleen Fulmer, in the cassette collection and book *Her Wings Unfurled* through heartbeats catlogue.org, © 1989, Colleen Fulmer.

Response to the Word:
Ritual of the Stations of the Cross

LECTOR 2

A reading from the Prophet Isaiah (42:1–4, 52:13–15, with "he" made plural):

> Here are my servants, whom I uphold,
> My chosen, in whom my soul delights;
> I have put my spirit upon them;
> they will bring forth justice to the nations.
> They will not cry or lift up their voices,
> or make them heard in the street;
> a bruised reed they will not break,
> and a dimly burning wick they will not quench;
> they will faithfully bring forth justice.
> They will not grow faint or be crushed
> until they have established justice in the earth;
> and the coastlands wait for their teaching. . . .
> See, my servants shall prosper;
> they shall be exalted and lifted up,
> and shall be very high.
> Just as there were many who were astonished at them—
> so marred were their appearances, beyond human semblance,
> and their form beyond that of mortals—
> so they shall startle many nations;
> kings shall shut their mouths because of them;
> for that which had not been told them they shall see,
> and that which they had not heard they shall contemplate.

"And they recognized him."

Invitation to Participate in the Stations of the Cross

The leader invites everyone to participate in each station by standing and bowing to the Cross, as able, and then sitting during each reflection, silence, and response. The leader proclaims each station.

THE FIRST STATION: JESUS IS CONDEMNED TO DEATH

Ita: Archbishop Oscar Romero knew what was in store. He was gunned down at Mass on March 24, 1980, but not before he pronounced these words. "Christ invites us not to fear persecution because, believe me, brothers and sisters, one who is committed to the poor must face the same fate as the poor. And in El Salvador we know what the fate of the poor signifies: to disappear, to be tortured, to be captive and to be found dead."[21] On December 1, 1980, I would choose to read those words. It was at a prayer service, the last night of a Maryknoll conference in Nicaragua. It was to be my last supper.

Silence

Response: O Christ, rejected one, we adore you and bless you; by your holy cross, help us transform our world.

THE SECOND STATION: JESUS TAKES UP THE CROSS

Maura: It was late August, 1980. I barely had time to become acquainted with my new work with Ita in Chalatenango when an ominous threat appeared on the door of the parish house. A sign was tacked to the entrance. On it was drawn a knife and a head, dripping with blood, and these words, "Anyone entering here will be killed." A chill came over me, but I chose to enter in.

Response: O Christ, gateway to life, we adore you and bless you; by your holy cross, help us transform our world.

THE THIRD STATION:
JESUS FALLS THE FIRST TIME

Ita: Dear Rene: It's early September, and Carla's death is still so fresh. And I'm still hurting so much. "Of course I've been angry and I felt it was such a stupidity. It's much more than having a friend die—because Carla was friend, coworker . . . and maybe more important at times, sister and sharer of a faith and vision in the midst of so much violence, hate and death.

"I can't answer logically the struggle we have in front of sickness, human limits, and mystery. . . . Maybe we rage against the things/events we can't control because we're scared, and it shows just where our power ends and where we have to hang on in faith or else throw in the towel. Because whether it's a flash flood or a weird virus or whatever—there's a lot of things beyond us."[22]

Silence

Response: O Christ, vulnerable one, we adore you and bless you; by your holy cross, help us transform our world.

THE FOURTH STATION:
JESUS MEETS HIS MOTHER

Ita: Dear Mom: "You probably know that Maura Clarke will be coming out to Chalatenango. Maura is a tremendous woman, has a lot of experience in Nicaragua, and has been home for the last three or four years doing Mission Education. She is very Irish and has a huge, loving, warm heart. I think she's going to be fantastic for all these people who come in who are traumatized, or who have been hiding, scared for their

"And they recognized him."

lives—I just think Maura's going to be God's gift to them."[23]

Silence

Response: O Christ, our Mother, laboring on the cross for us,[24] we adore you and bless you; by your holy cross, help us transform our world.

THE FIFTH STATION:
SIMON HELPS JESUS CARRY THE CROSS

Jean: I arrived in La Libertad on August 10, 1979. By then, El Salvador was a very dangerous place, as "the country drifted deeper into chaos."[25] But it was clear to me: the people needed support. So, it seemed like the perfect time for me to be here.[26] And then something happened. I began to realize that the very people I had come to serve had something I wanted and needed. They knew about life and suffering, about courage and human dignity, about friendship and solidarity. I would learn from them.

Silence

Response: O Christ, our help in ages past, we adore you and bless you; by your holy cross, help us transform our world.

THE SIXTH STATION:
VERONICA WIPES THE FACE OF JESUS

Ita: A woman came to me asking if I would accompany her to the site where the bodies of two young men had been found, to determine whether or not one of them was her son. So we got into the parish Jeep and set out to find the farmer who had buried them. Confronted with the mother's anguished uncertainty over the fate of her son, he finally agreed to help us. Making a small opening in the fresh grave, he dug down just far enough to reveal a white cloth with which he had covered the face of the dead boy: when he raised the cloth, the mother looked down onto the face of her son and said very quietly, "Now I know where my son lies. I know he is with God and now, I just want him to rest here."[27] The image of that face haunts me.

Silence

Response: O Christ, human face of God, we adore you and bless you; by your holy cross, help us transform our world.

THE SEVENTH STATION:
JESUS STUMBLES A SECOND TIME

Dorothy: October 21, 1980. Dear Martha: Jean and I spend our days on rescue mission after rescue mission. Today there was a tiny newborn fellow, six days old, "just an itty-bitty skinny little thing . . . but so cute. . . . My heart just aches for these people, when I see what they've got to work with. And they're really hoping to win. I just don't know how in God's name they're going to do it. We [the U.S.] give money for communication equipment and huge trucks and such so the military can get up there easier to kill them. . . It just makes me ill when I see us doing this kind of garbage."[28]

Silence

Response: O Christ, suffering servant, we adore you and bless you; by your holy cross, help us transform our world.

MUSIC

Sung Refrain: "Behold the Wood," text and tune by Dan Schutte, © 1976, Daniel L. Schutte and New Dawn Music.

THE EIGHTH STATION:
THE WOMEN OF JERUSALEM WEEP FOR JESUS

Maura: Dear friends: "The way innocent people, families, children are cut up with machetes and blessed temples of the Lord thrown and left for the buzzards to feed on them seems unbelievable, but it happens every day. . . .

WALKING WITH WISDOM'S DAUGHTERS

"*And they recognized him.*"

We don't know how long this can continue, but the pain goes on and there are many hungry people hiding and struggling. . . . The courage . . . of these people never ceases to call me."[29]

Ita: "We keep plugging along here, because life is threatened by other evils worse than death—hatred, manipulation, vengeance, selfishness."[30]

Silence

Response: O Christ, lamenting one, we adore you and bless you; by your holy cross, help us transform our world.

THE NINTH STATION: JESUS FALLS THE THIRD TIME

Dorothy: Dear President Carter: "I am a North American missionary working in . . . El Salvador. I have been here for six years, and I have seen the oppression of the people grow worse each year." But, do you have any idea how many innocent people are being killed, with American equipment? One old man was coming down the road with three cows—he got killed. One young man was going to wash down by the well—he got killed. One young girl about twelve years old had in her hands the words of a song which had been written in honor of one of the priests who had been martyred."[31] She got killed. What do you think of this situation, Mr. President?

Silence

Response: O Christ, innocent, crucified one, we adore you and bless you; by your holy cross, help us transform our world.

THE TENTH STATION: JESUS IS STRIPPED OF HIS GARMENTS

Maura: "These [Salvadorans] are the most rugged, browned, simple and faith-filled men and women who are religious leaders of their various pueblos. It takes courage for them to continue any celebration of the Word or meetings because anyone suspected of being in an organization or attached to the Church is in serious danger. . . . The poor really strip you, pull you, challenge you, evangelize you, show you God. . . ."[32]

Silence

Response: O Christ, Our Way, Our Truth, and Our Life, we adore you and bless you; by your holy cross, help us transform our world.

THE ELEVENTH STATION: JESUS IS NAILED TO THE CROSS
. . . .

Jean: Last month I went through the agony of the garden and finally came to deep peace. Now it is mid November. "The Peace Corps left today, and my heart sank low. The danger is extreme and they are right to leave. . . . Now I must assess my own position, because I am not up for suicide. Several times I have decided to leave—I almost could except for the children, the poor bruised victims of adult lunacy. Who would care for them? Whose heart would be so staunch as to favor the reasonable thing in a sea of their tears and loneliness? Not mine, dear friend, not mine."[33]

Silence

Response: O Christ, compassion poured out, we adore you and bless you; by your holy cross, help us transform our world.

THE TWELFTH STATION: JESUS DIES ON THE CROSS
. . . .

Narrator: It is December 1. In Managua, Maryknoll Sisters are ending their Conference in prayer. In Chalatenango, the parish sacristan is approached and shown a death list by a stranger. The names of Sisters Maura Clarke and Ita Ford are on that list. When Jean and Dorothy pick them up at the airport the following evening, they

"And they recognized him."

are watched by National Guardsmen . . . followed . . . stopped . . . brutally raped . . . killed . . . and buried together by the side of the road.

Silence

Response: O Christ, blessed and Broken, we adore you and bless you; by your holy cross, help us transform our world.

THE THIRTEENTH STATION:
JESUS IS TAKEN DOWN FROM THE CROSS

Narrator: They all knew well the passion that had brought them here. Ita's voice still speaks to us of that passion in an August letter to her niece. "Dear Jennifer, It's your six-teenth birthday, and I want you to know how much I love you. What I want to say, some of it isn't too jolly birthday talk, but it's real. . . . The reasons why so many people are being killed are quite complicated, yet there are some clear, simple strands. One is that many people have found a meaning to live, to sacrifice, to struggle and even die. And whether their life spans sixteen years, sixty or ninety, for them their life has had a purpose. . . . What I'm saying is that I hope you can come to find that which gives life a deep meaning for you, something that energizes you, enthuses you . . . I can't tell you what it might be. That's for you to choose, to love. I can just encourage you to start looking and support you in the search."[34]

Silence

Response: O Christ, passionate one, we adore you and bless you; by your holy cross, help us transform our world.

THE FOURTEENTH STATION:
JESUS IS LAID IN THE TOMB

Narrator: American ambassador Robert White watched as the disfigured bodies of the four women were lifted from their roadside grave. The bodies of Jean Donovan and Dorothy Kazel were delivered home to their parents for burial. Maura Clarke and Ita Ford were laid to rest among their people in Chalatenango.

Silence

Response: O Christ, home for the outcast, we adore you and bless you; by your holy cross, help us transform our world.

THE FIFTEENTH STATION: THE RESURRECTION

Narrator: Father Jon Sobrino said this. "The murdered Christ is here in the person of four women. . . . But he is risen, too, in these same four women. . . . Salvation comes to us through all women and men who love truth more than lies, who are more eager to give than receive, and whose love is that supreme love that gives life rather than keeping it for oneself."[35]

Silence

Response: O Christ, living one, we adore you and bless you; by your holy cross, help us transform our world.

SIGN OF THE CROSS

The leader invites everyone to pair up and sign one another with God's power of compassion poured out, of life out of death, as she proclaims, "My friend, receive the sign of the cross on your forehead. It is Christ who now strengthens you with this sign of his love. Learn to know and follow him."[36]

CLOSING HYMN

"Pan de Vida," text by Bob Hurd and Pia Moriarty, based on Galatians 3:28–29, tune by Bob Hurd, © 1988, OCP Publications.

"And they recognized him."

Four Women Who Walked
the Way of the Cross

We all have our personal struggles. With family, perhaps. Or work. Or illness and loss. Or getting in touch with the passion of our lives. Then, coming to terms with living out that passion. Oftentimes it's hard to see the big picture, when we're in the midst of the struggle.

However, once in a while we're given perspective. Time has gone by, and meaning is being made of something very significant. So it is with the stories of these four women: Maura Clarke, Dorothy Kazel, Ita Ford and Jean Donovan. As I write these words, we are fast approaching the twenty-fifth anniversary of their death. We are also approaching another significant anniversary, the fortieth anniversary of the last document to emerge from the Second Vatican Council (on December 7). Entitled *Gaudium et Spes,* or *Joy and Hope,* this lavishly Spirit-filled pronouncement is often called, with good reason, *The Pastoral Constitution on the Church in the Modern World.* The point is this. The church has much to offer our world whenever it is authentic to its mission of bringing Christ to life today. At the same time, the church has much to learn from the world. And the church is at its best when it is in continual dialogue with the people of the world, "reading the signs of the times" according to gospel values.

In order to do justice to the telling of these four courageous lives, it is essential to situate them within the dramatic events surrounding them (like the outpouring of God's Holy Spirit at the Second Vatican Council and the resulting Medellin Conference of Latin American bishops). It is also important to give a "feel" for the land, the immediate history, and the people they loved so deeply. As a result, the essay is longer than the others, but it is worth the read. Because the book cannot accommodate this length, the article can be found on the web site.

To my way of thinking, it is no accident that these two anniversaries fall at the beginning of Advent. For, in Advent starkness, we are called to authenticity as God's People. In Advent darkness, we are called to actively watch and wait, that we might see and become the words that one of our Advent psalms (85:10) proclaims: "Steadfast love and faithfulness will meet; righteousness and peace will kiss each other." Such becoming is what the lives of Maura Clarke, Dorothy Kazel, Ita Ford and Jean Donovan were all about. Such becoming is the call on our lives, as well.

A fuller account of the lives and events surrounding the deaths of these four courageous women can be found on the website http://avemariapress.com/itemdetail.cfm?nItemid=780

SOME RESOURCES

Brett, Donna Whitson and Edward T. Brett. *Murdered in Central America: The Stories of Eleven U.S. Missionaries.* Maryknoll, N.Y.: Orbis Books, 1988.

Carrigan, Ana. *Salvador Witness: The Life and Calling of Jean Donovan.* New York: Simon and Schuster, 1984.

Kazel, Dorothy Capon. *Alleluia Woman: Sister Dorothy Kazel, OSU.* Cleveland: Chapel Publications, 1987.

McLaughlin, Janice, "Four Heroic Lives End in Martyrdom," in *National Catholic Reporter*, December 19, 1980, pp. 1, 27–29.

Noone, Judith M., M.M. *The Same Fate as the Poor.* Maryknoll, N.Y.: Maryknoll Sisters, 1984.

Royal, Robert. *The Catholic Martyrs of the Twentieth Century.* New York: The Crossroad Publishing Company, 2000.

Sobrino, Jon. *Spirituality of Liberation: Toward Political Holiness.* Trans. from the Spanish by Robert R. Barr. Maryknoll, N.Y.: Orbis Books, 1988.

NOTES

1. This prayer service was inspired by the work of our storytelling group, Women of the Well, in creating a liturgical drama on these four women. It is called, "Certain Women."

2. I prefer "certain" women to "some women" in the NRSV translation of 8:2; either is an accurate translation of the Greek.

3. Luke 24:6–7.

"And they recognized him."

4. Moises Sandoval, "Four Heroic Lives End in Martyrdom: Clarke," *National Catholic Reporter*, December 19, 1980, 28, as found in Donna Whitson Brett and Edward, *Murdered in Cental America: The Stories of Eleven U.S. Missionaries* (Maryknoll, N.Y.: Orbis Books, 1988), 276; this was the remembrance of a sister with whom she ministered. This book will hereafter be noted as Brett.

5. Remembrances of Dorothy Kazel by Sr. Kathleen Cooney, as found in Brett, p. 200.

6. Remembrances of Dorothy Kazel by Sr. James Francis, as found in Brett, p. 200.

7. Remembrances of Sr. Dorothy Kazel by her good friend and colleague in El Salvador, Sr. Martha Owen, as found in Brett, p. 200.

8. Brett, p. 197.

9. Sheila Phelan, quoted in "Life of Love," p. 7, as found in Brett, p. 201.

10. Brett, p. 255, quoting from Judith M. Noone, M.M., *The Same Fate as the Poor*, (Maryknoll, N.Y.: Maryknoll Sisters, 1984), 20. Noone's book will hereafter be noted as Noone.

11. Brett, p. 214.

12. Brett, p. 216.

13. Letter from Sr. Carla Piette to Cecelia Vandal, M.M., 14 May 1980, MSA: C73, as found in Noone, p. 92. At the time, there were about 550 people per square mile in this smallest nation of Central America.

14. Brett, p. 281.

15. Notes from an eight-day retreat in 1976, as found in Noone, p. 75.

16. Brett, p. 256.

17. Ibid.

18. Brett, p. 263.

19. Brett, p. 218.

20. Liturgical reflection by Sr. Sheila Tobbe on December 14, 1980, as found in Brett, p. 229.

21. From Oscar Romero's homily on February 17, 1980, as found in Brett, p. 300.

22. Ita's letter to her sister Rene, early September 1980, as found in Ana Carrigan, *Salvador Witness: The Life and Calling of Jean Donovan* (New York: Simon and Schuster, 1984), 199.

23. Letter from Ita to her mother, as found in Carrigan, p. 194.

24. This is an image from Julian of Norwich, *Showings* LT 63, 298.

25. Carrigan, p. 91.

26. Carrigan, p. 92.

27. Carrigan, p. 224.

28. Dorothy Kazel, tape to Sr. Martha Owen, October 21, 1980, as found in Brett, p. 243.

29. Maura Clarke, letter to Margaret Dillon, M.M., November 22, 1980, and to Patricia Haggerty, November 20, 1980, as found in Brett, p. 297.

30. Ita Ford, letter to Jean Reardon Baumann, October 27, 1980, as found in Brett, p. 297.

31. Dorothy Kazel's letter to President Carter late in October 1980, as found in Brett, pp. 244–45.

32. Letter to Mary Manning, 11 August 1980, MSA:M 188, as found in Noone, pp. 115–16.

33. Letter of Jean to a friend, as found in Brett, p. 252.

34. Ita Ford's letter to her niece, Jennifer Sullivan, August 16, 1980, as found in Brett, p. 274.

35. Jon Sobrino, *Spirituality of Liberation: Toward Political Holiness*, trans. from the Spanish by Robert R. Barr (Maryknoll, N.Y.: Orbis Books, 1988), 156.

36. These words are slightly adapted from the ritual, "Acceptance into the Order of Catechumens," Rite of Christian Initiation for Adults.

"And they recognized him."

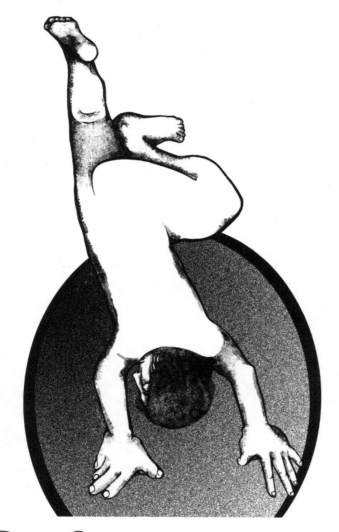

seven

Woman Re-membered

From Lament to Hope

We Remember and Resist Violence Against Women

This is a service of healing and hope. But healing begins by naming—and lamenting—the pain. Hope lies in recognizing that God's Spirit cries out with these women for healing and justice. The stories of lament in this service are all true, representing diversity across time and culture. They are intended to move us toward intercession to our God and to imagination of God's future with and for us.

Everyone is wounded. But a number of participants at this liturgy may have been profoundly wounded in body and spirit. Therefore, it is essential to offer a warm, welcoming, safe space for worship. Candlelight is everywhere—in the gathering space and in the worship space. Greeters offer participants a warm welcome, a program, and an unlighted candle.

A couple of tables in the gathering space are set up with information on violence against women, such as information about local shelters, and other local efforts to combat such violence. Also included might be the 1992 statement by the United States Conference of Catholic Bishops, "When I Call for Help: Domestic Violence Against Women."[1]

The worship space is welcoming. In the center of the worship space is a table with plants, water, and a large candle, symbolic of life. On one side, near the people, is space for the musicians. On the other side is the presider's chair and lectern, with the scripture. Candles are placed around the worship space. Voices and readers will come from the assembly.

Ministers: *the prayer leader, readers, voices, musicians, and cantor*

Materials: *candles (one large), programs, table, plants, water, presider's chair, lectern, scripture*

Gathering Rites

WELCOME

The leader introduces the nature of the healing prayer and provides another warm welcome, setting the tone for a time of honesty and hope.

CALL TO WORSHIP

Leader: All who come here wounded . . .

All: Cry out with the Spirit of God!

Leader: All who come here in fear, anxiety, doubt, depression . . .

All: Cry out with the Spirit of God!

Leader: All who come here healed, at one with people in pain . . .

All: Cry out with the Spirit of God!

Leader: All who come here in hope, speaking truth in love, seeking justice, compassion and healing for all . . .

"And they recognized him."

All: Cry out with the Spirit of God, who is Hope, Truth, Love, Justice, Compassion, and Wounded Healer.

OPENING HYMN
. . . .

"God of Day and God of Darkness," text by Marty Haugen, tune is BEACH SPRING, © 1985, GIA Publications, Inc., verses 1–3.

or

"Spirit Blowing Through Creation," text and tune by Marty Haugen, © 1987, GIA Publications, Inc.

Stories of Lament
. . . .

READING: JEREMIAH 31:15
. . . .

PSALM 22
. . . .

"My God, My God," text by Marty Haugen, based on Psalm 22:8–9, 17–18, 19–20, 23–24 (refrain trans. © 1969, ICEL); tune by Marty Haugen, © 1983, GIA Publications, Inc. The musical refrain may be sung after each of the following voices. Or, people may recite the words "Rachel is weeping for her children because they are no more."

Voice 1:   I live in the suburbs. I had no idea that one of my best friends was being abused until one night, late. The phone jolted me awake in the wee hours of the morning. It was my friend, sobbing, "I need your help— right away! The children and I are in a phone booth. Can you pick us up, now?" I got into the car and raced to the phone booth, where my friend and her children were huddled together in their pajamas. Her husband had flown into a drunken rage, trying to kill her with a hunting arrow. Their oldest son had intervened, only to become the target of her husband's rage. But her husband was so drunk that she was able to get all of them out of the house.

I took them home and heard my friend's story of abuse at the hands of an alcoholic husband. They were both so active in the church. Who would ever have imagined such a thing? The next day, I took her to the parish priest. And he advised her to go back home! Instead, I got her some help from a friend, who is a religious sister. Counseling, first for her, then for him . . . followed by Al-Anon and AA. In their case, there is hope.[2]

Refrain, sung or recited by all.

Voice 2: My name is Tamar, and I was not even safe in a royal palace. It did not matter that I was a daughter of King David, the beloved king of Israel. It did not matter that I was a virgin, beautiful and wise. It did not matter that I pleaded my case well, relying on the laws of my people. It did not matter . . . for I was a woman, living in fear of my half brother Amnon. King David, my very own father, ordered me into Amnon's bedroom, without knowing my brother's evil pretense. Amnon attacked me. After that he hated me, with a hatred that is the underside of lust. He put me out, now used, abused, and wasted in the eyes of my people. The only compassion I knew came from my brother Absalom; he kept me in his house, but I remained "desolate" the rest of my life.[3]

Refrain, sung or recited by all.

Voice 3: I am a Muslim woman from Bosnia. I was enslaved just a few short years ago. I was gang raped, held in a "rape camp" during the Bosnian war, after Serbian forces butchered their way through our town of Foca. I was tortured. We never knew when the soldiers would come and say, "You . . . and you . . . and you." The nightmares will never go away. But, justice is happening. On February 22, 2001, three of these Serbian commanders were convicted of crimes against humanity by a United Nations war crimes tribunal for what they did to us. The world must continue to watch . . . the world must continue to see . . . the world must continue to act.[4]

Refrain, sung or recited by all.

"And they recognized him."

Voice 4:   I am a Roman Catholic sister. My name is "Laura," and I was seventeen when I entered a diocesan convent in West Africa.[5] In my culture, everybody looks up to priests. "You are made to feel that if you talk [about their misdeeds] you are being disloyal."[6] But, our novice mistress had "warned us that after we took our vows the priests would be all over us. . . . She said it would be our choice to keep our vows."[7] But I had no idea what a nightmare it would be. Some of the other sisters told me their stories because they knew I was angry at what was going on. "The priests were always asking us for sex. . . ."[8]

And then it happened to me, at age twenty-seven. I was on a pastoral assignment with a priest I knew well. It was to a remote village, and we were to return the same day. But it rained, in torrents, and we needed to stay overnight. We were in an empty building, separated that night by a long hallway. But during the night he came and forced himself on me. I protested throughout, but to no avail. Afterwards, I was forlorn that "it was in the religious life that I broke my virginity."[9] Now I have left religious life, but intend to live out my vocation as a lay Catholic.

Refrain, sung or recited by all.

Voice 5:   I am the only one who can speak the unspeakable, the depraved horror. For she is no more. And the horror might have been mine, as well . . . I was that close. I am the only daughter of an old Ephraimite, you see, a virgin. And this night began in our town square of Gibeah. My old father came upon a Levite and his servant and concubine—this woman who is no more. They were on their way from Bethlehem in Judah to the remote hill country of Ephraim and needed hospitality for the night. Nobody in the whole town had taken them in, so my father offered them bed and board. The woman—I still don't know her name—told me her story while the men ate and drank. She had become angry with the Levite and left him, returning to her father's house in Bethlehem. Four months later, he came after her, saying he would "speak tenderly to her and bring her back."[10] Well, he brought her back, all right, but there was no tenderness. Even from her own father, who was willing to let her go.

Her story was interrupted by loud pounding on the door. And in rapid succession, an exchange of words . . . and people. Perverse men from the city, demanding the Levite, to abuse him. My father, refusing, horrified at their violation of hospitality. Then offering two women instead. My father, offering the concubine and me, his very own daughter! "Do whatever you want to them."[11] As I gasped, the Levite shoved his concubine outside, alone, to satisfy their greed for violence. (*Pause*) We found her in the morning with one hand draped over the doorstep, a human plea for sanity and justice.

But, the attack continued, even then. She was "despised and rejected . . . stricken . . . like a lamb that is led to the slaughter, and like a sheep that before its shearers is silent, so [s]he did not open [her] mouth."[12] Innocent, her body was broken, cut apart and sent throughout all of Israel. Had the gang killed her? Or was that final demented deed done by her "husband," who violated her beyond recognition? I'll never know. I only know I can't get near any man or trust any man, especially my father. "Has such a thing ever happened since the day that the Israelites came up from the land of Egypt until this day? Consider it, take counsel, and speak out."[13]

> *Refrain, sung or recited by all.*
>
> *Silence*

Prayer of Petition

MUSICAL REFLECTION

"In Her Poor," text and tune by Colleen Fulmer, in the cassette collection and book *Her Wings Unfurled*, available through www.heartbeatscatlogue.org. *This hymn is most appropriate here because it speaks of God waiting and crying out in Her poor, in those most in need.*

READING: ROMANS 8:22–27

INVITATION TO PRAYER BY THE LEADER

God prays in us, agonizes with us, cries out for human justice. God is like Rachel, weeping because her children are no more. Take a moment now with this God and bring your needs to her. Listen for any movement of God's Spirit within you, as we prepare to pray together.

Response after each petition: "God-with-us, heal us."

- For the healing of anyone who has been abused physically, emotionally, economically, spiritually, or in any other way, we pray . . .

- For those who help heal the wounds of violence, we pray . . .

- For all who resist the evil of abuse that would destroy minds and bodies and devour souls, we pray . . .

- For all survivors, that their strength may only increase, we pray . . .

- For friends and supporters of the wounded, we pray . . .

- For the increased will in church and society to call abusers to accountability, we pray . . .

- For what else shall we pray?

Ritual of Transforming Hope

HYMN

"You Are Mine," text and tune by David Haas, © 1991, GIA Publications, Inc.

READING: ISAIAH 49:8–9A, 14–17.

NAMING OF HOPES AND DREAMS BY THE LEADER

God has promised to be with us and for us. God has further promised to stir up hope in our midst. For God has said, "Then afterward I will pour out my spirit on all flesh; your sons and your daughters shall prophesy, your old men [and women] shall dream dreams, and your young [women and] men shall see visions."[14] Would anyone who has been so inspired, please share your vision, hope, or dream with us now? *Note: Those who participated as the "Voices" will have been invited to begin this process.*

INVITATION TO CANDLE LIGHTING BY THE LEADER:

To "seal" these hopes and dreams, each person is invited to come forward to the large candle, drawing light for their own candles and lives, and then return to their own place.

MUSIC DURING THE RITUAL

"Shepherd Me, O God," text by Marty Haugen, based on Psalm 23, tune by Marty Haugen, © 1986, GIA Publications, Inc., and the music only from "You Are Mine," if needed.

"And they recognized him."

Closing Rites

● ●

BLESSING
● ● ● ● ● ● ●

Leader: God keeps promises. For through Jesus, God has given us an Advocate, the Spirit of Truth, to be with us always.

All: O Spirit of Truth, Advocate for Life, Lover and Friend, heal and guide us, encourage us with strength, love, and wisdom. Permeate us with the power to do your work, both now and forevermore. Amen!

CLOSING HYMN
● ● ● ● ● ● ● ● ● ● ●

"Prayer of Peace," based on a Navajo prayer, text and tune by David Haas, © 1987, GIA Publications, Inc.

SIGN OF PEACE
● ● ● ● ● ● ● ● ● ●

Violence Against Women

● ●

Suffering can be redemptive, like that of Jesus, when chosen freely out of love, out of passion for human life, out of a God-given mission. But there is suffering that is not redemptive, like suffering at the hand of those who bludgeon life, bearing the telltale fingerprints of evil. This kind of suffering can take many forms, one of which is violence against women. To this kind of suffering, we say, "No! Never again!" Not returning violence for violence. But remembering, lamenting, and firmly resisting, with conviction.

Violence against women is everywhere: in city and suburb, on the farm and in small towns, in every nation of the world. It is perpetrated against women of every color, size, age, race, and economic background. It happens among Catholics, Jews, Muslims, and Protestants of every tradition; it happens among people of faith everywhere. It is estimated that one in four women "has been raped or beaten or has experienced incest. Nearly one in every three adult women experiences at least one physical assault by a partner during adulthood. . . . According to the platform of the Fourth United Nations World Conference on Women held in Beijing in 1995, family violence is epidemic in most societies around the globe."[15]

Violence against women is also found in scripture. We have only to recall the rape of Dinah, the only daughter among Judah's thirteen children.[16] Or the story of Hagar: surrogate mother against her will and outcast in the wilderness, by order of Sarah with the consent of Abraham.[17] Or the rape of Tamar, daughter of King David, by her half-brother Amnon.[18] Or the exile of Queen Vashti, wife of King Ahasuerus, who refused the king's command to show off her beauty before a party of men "merry with wine."[19] The king retaliated, at the advice of his ministers, by banishing her from his sight forever, "declaring that every man should be master in his own house."[20] Or the death of Jephthah's daughter, his only child, because of a foolish, faithless vow made by her father.[21] Or Lot's betrayal of his two virgin daughters. It seems that all the depraved men of Sodom were intent on raping Lot's two male guests. Lot refused that horrific request but offered up his precious daughters instead. They were only saved by the actions of the guests, who struck all the men blind.[22] Or, finally, the gang rape, murder, and dismemberment of the concubine from Bethlehem, "the most sinned against" woman in all of scripture.[23] More will be said momentarily of her story.

In recent years, safe havens have developed as places of shelter, restoration, and a second start. Often these shelters become places of education and advocacy as well. It is primarily out of their work that we more fully understand the nature of violence against women. Most often, perhaps, physical battering comes to mind when people think of violence against women. And indeed, that kind of violence occurs far too often. But violence can take other forms, and all are aspects of what has become known as the "power and control wheel."[24] In an effort to control another person, an abuser might use any or all of four other kinds of abuse, as well. There is psychological abuse, which attempts to instill fear. How?

"And they recognized him."

Through intimidation, blackmail, mind games, continual "checking up" on the other, isolating the other from friends, even destroying pets and property. There is emotional abuse, which uses any number of ways to annihilate another's self-worth (e.g., constant criticism, yelling, silent treatment, put downs). There is economic abuse, which attempts to make another economically dependent. There is sexual abuse, which coerces another into sexual contact without consent. Yes, there is such a thing as marital rape.

Even given all this abuse, leaving the situation may be the most difficult thing a woman has ever done.[25] The danger in leaving is not to be minimized; for it is then that the abuser might become most violent, to her and even to any children involved. It is most important that the woman who is attempting to leave the situation understands her options and plans ahead. She needs to know about shelters in her area. She needs to know the depth of support from local and state systems. And if she is a woman of faith, she needs to know that God never intends for her to live in abuse. Unfortunately, some religious leaders have sent women back into a violent situation too many times. But God does not condone abuse. And this brings us back to a confrontation with scripture.

THE CONCUBINE FROM BETHLEHEM

This woman's story is sadistic and brutal beyond belief. First of all, the questions must be asked: What do we make of such violence in scripture? And what are we to do with it? Scripture scholar Gina Hens-Piazza offers us some penetrating reflection on that question, in looking at the violence so deeply imbedded in the Books of Joshua and Judges, for example.[26] We are far too often tempted to ignore the violence and remove it from our screen of consideration. But, that does not make the violence go away, and it leaves our questions unanswered. Another temptation might be to turn primarily to the New Testament, leaving behind any violent stories of the Hebrew scriptures altogether. But, this approach can rightly seem to denigrate the Hebrew scriptures, adding fuel to centuries of damaging anti-Semitism. And, such an approach ignores the ways in which Christian scripture has been used to promote forms of violence. For example, the "Christianized" Roman household codes—as found in Colossians and Ephesians—have been used to justify slavery and the domination of women by men.[27] While disagreement remains over the value of these codes, scholars can agree that they do reflect the culture of the first century. The question remains, how might we profitably deal with such violence? First, we need to attempt an understanding of the times and the purposes of the author in setting down such stories. Second, and this is very important, we need to remember the victims *in memoriam*.[28] Along with this, we must read the story as a documentation of "the case against violence and its perpetrators."[29] This puts us on the lookout for violence in our own society, and even in our hearts. Also, we must consider how people from diverse communities might read the story. The story will read very differently for an indigenous group that has been violated, for example, as opposed to a group that has most typically been "in power." In the end, these stories are our stories, meant in some way to be a call to conversion.

Back to the concubine. Her story takes place, the author tells us, "when there was no king in Israel."[30] These few words form a refrain, stated earlier and then again, at the very end of the book, "In those days there was no king in Israel; all the people did what was right in their own eyes."[31] We are alerted. Chaos reigns and something evil is about to take place. Like so many other women in scripture, she is given no name. Like so many other women in scripture, she is an object from the very beginning, "taken" as a "concubine" by "a certain Levite."[32] She never speaks, though she does take action, twice. The first time is almost immediately. The NRSV translation, following the Greek and Old Latin, tells us that she "became angry" at the Levite and went to her father's house in Bethlehem. But the ancient Hebrew text says it this way: "his concubine played the harlot," then returned to her father's house.[33] In any case, after four months, the Levite "set out after her, to speak tenderly to her and bring her back."[34] Those words remind us of words spoken by a compassionate God to an unfaithful Israel, through the prophet Hosea.[35] We are set up to expect this Levite, a man of the tribe of Moses, Aaron, and Miriam, to treat this woman well. And the story begins to unfold, in two acts.

The first act takes place in her father's house. But the concubine fades into the background, since all the action takes place between the two men, the Levite and his father-in-law. The hospitality of her father has everything to do with male bonding and then with male competition. Whose will prevails in the exchanges between

"And they recognized him."

them? Ultimately, the Levite is the winner, taking off with the concubine and his servant toward the end of the fifth day. No tender words have been spoken; she remains an object in the eyes of both. Furthermore, danger is in the air. As they approach Jebus (which would later become known as Jerusalem), Levite and servant debate about where to spend the night. Again, the woman has nothing to say. It is the Levite who decides; they will go on to Gibeah because "we will not turn aside into a city of foreigners, who do not belong to the people of Israel."[36]

Act two takes place that night in Gibeah; it becomes a night of unspeakable terror. At first, nobody welcomes them in. Then an old man from Ephraim, the home territory of the Levite, comes forward to extend hospitality. They are all safely inside his house until some "men of the city, a perverse lot," surround the house, and start "pounding on the door."[37] The men demand sex with the Levite, in striking similarity to the story of Lot's betrayal of his two daughters. For this old man from Ephraim is also willing to sacrifice his very own virgin daughter and the Levite's concubine to satisfy the men's evil intentions. This time, the guest is not a savior. In fact, it is the Levite himself who shoves his own concubine out into the night, to be ravaged, raped, and violated all night long. Her only other action is to make her way to the doorway of the house in the wee hours of the morning. She is found with one hand draped piteously over the doorway. Is she dead? We don't know. Mercifully, for what follows, we can only hope that she is.

The evil escalates to a rapid conclusion. The Levite presumably started out on a mission to "speak tenderly" to his concubine. Yet after this night of horror, all he can say to her is this, "Get up. . . we are going."[38] He tosses her on his donkey and sets out for home. Immediately upon arriving, "he took a knife," not unlike Abraham taking a knife to Isaac.[39] This time no angel intervenes; the Levite "cut her into twelve pieces, limb by limb, and sent her throughout all the territory of Israel."[40] "Her body was broken and given to many."[41] That pronouncement by Phyllis Trible at the beginning of her commentary on this woman's story serves as both judgment and as connection to another innocent, "like a lamb that is led to the slaughter . . . so he did not open his mouth."[42]

This brutality begets more brutality. And it is violence of gigantic proportions. "All the Israelites came out, from Dan to Beer-sheba" to give the Levite a hearing in the matter of "this criminal act."[43] Sure of himself, the Levite places the entire blame of this "vile outrage" on the Benjaminites of Gibeah.[44] The result? "Outrage erupts at the harm done to *a man through his property* but ignores the violence done against the woman herself."[45] The tribes demand that the Benjaminites hand over "those scoundrels in Gibeah, so that we may put them to death, and purge the evil from Israel."[46] The tribe of Benjamin refuses and is slaughtered by their kin; only six hundred men escape into the wilderness. In remorse that one of their tribes has been nearly blotted out, the Israelites have compassion on Benjamin. But they face a dilemma, for they have all vowed that none of their women will marry a Benjaminite. Their solution is one that wreaks yet more violence on women. For they discover "four hundred young virgins who had never slept with a man" and bring them to the camp at Shiloh.[47] Then they urge the remaining men of Benjamin to abduct these virgins during the festival of the Lord there and take them as wives, like prime property. And it is done, with the final reminder, "In those days there was no king in Israel; all the people did what was right in their own eyes."

The question remains, what are we to do with this story of total violence against this concubine? We do know this. In the original context, the author was making a strong case for the establishment of a monarchy. But scripture scholars Johanna Stiebert and Jerome T. Walsh offer us a warning, in response. "There are no 'inspired' political systems; . . . if we are not under God's control, we are under no one's, not even our own."[48] Those who shaped the canon of scripture probably have yet another "take" on this story. In judgment on the depravity of those days, they immediately followed this final story of Judges with that of an honorable woman of courage. The Hebrew Bible follows this story with the story of Hannah, as found at the beginning of 1 Samuel. Hannah is a faith-filled woman in deep distress, for she is barren. So she prays openly before God in the Temple for a son, vowing to return this son to God's service.[49] Not only that, she stands up for herself, when Eli the priest accuses her of being drunk (because she is moving her lips in prayer). In the tradition, Hannah is held up as a model for the intercessory prayer of the rabbis.[50] The Greek Bible inserts the story of yet another model of faith between these two. And that is the story of Ruth, an outsider who adopts the Hebrew God as her own, revealing God's steadfast love in the process. These faithful

"And they recognized him."

WALKING WITH WISDOM'S DAUGHTERS

women stand in judgment on the men of Israel. The prophet Hosea also renders judgment on them: "They have deeply corrupted themselves as in the days of Gibeah; God will remember their iniquity, he will punish their sins."[51] Finally, we as readers must render our own verdict, on them and on ourselves. In doing so, we might well be challenged by the words of the Levite (in a way he did not expect), regarding her story. "Consider it, take counsel, and speak out."[52] What shall we speak?

SOME RESOURCES

Fewell, Danna Nolan. "Judges," in *Women's Bible Commentary, Expanded Edition, With Apocrypha* edited by Carol A. Newsom and Sharon H. Ringe. Louisville, Ky.: Westminster John Knox Press, 1998, 73–83.

Fortune, Marie M. *Violence in the Family: A Worship Curriculum for Clergy and Other Helpers*. Cleveland: Pilgrim Press, 1991.

Hens-Piazza, Gina. "Violence in Joshua and Judges," in *The Bible Today*. Collegeville, Minn.: Liturgical Press, July/August 2001, 197–203.

National Conference of Catholic Bishops. *When I Call for Help: Domestic Violence Against Women*. Washington, D.C., 1992.

New York State Office for the Prevention of Domestic Violence. *Domestic Violence: Finding Safety and Support*. Rensselaer, New York: Capital View Office Park, 52 Washington Street, 3rd Floor, 1996. (518) 586-6262.

Stiebert, Johanna and Jerome T. Walsh. "Chaos Cries for a King," in *The Bible Today*. Collegeville, Minn.: Liturgical Press, July/August 2001, 211–215.

Trible, Phyllis. *Texts of Terror: Literary-Feminist Readings of Biblical Narratives*. Philadelphia: Fortress Press, 1984.

SOME ORGANIZATIONS

Texas Council on Family Violence, 8701 N. McPac Expressway, Suite 450, Austin, Texas 78759, (512) 794-1133.

The Center for the Prevention of Sexual and Domestic Violence, 936 North 34th Street, Suite 200, Seattle, Washington, 98103, (206) 634-1903.

The Clergy Partnership on Domestic Violence, Inc. P.O. Box 183, Madison, New Jersey 07940, (888) 245-9166.

U.S. Department of Justice: Office on Violence Against Women: www.usdoj.gov/ovw/help.htm.

NOTES
· · · · ·

1. This can be ordered from the United States Conference of Catholic Bishops or found in *Origins*, November 5, 1992, Vol. 22, No. 21.

2. This is a true story told by a friend.

3. Her story is told in 2 Samuel 13:1–22.

4. This story was told in the *Democrat and Chronicle*, Rochester, New York, February 23, 2001.

5. "Laura," not her real name, tells her story in the April 6, 2001, issue of *National Catholic Reporter*, hereafter referred to as NCR.

6. NCR, p. 4.

7. Ibid.

8. Ibid.

9. Ibid.

10. Judges 19:3.

11. Judges 19:24.

12. Isaiah 53:3, 4, 7b, c, d; this is the last of the "Suffering Servant Songs" of Isaiah. It is Phyllis Trible, in her *Texts of Terror: Literary-Feminist Readings of Biblical Narratives*, who suggests the comparison of this innocent woman's suffering with that of Jesus. Obviously, the daughter telling the story would not have said this, but the insight is worth expressing.

13. Judges 19:30; these words were originally spoken by the Levite, but reframe the story, as told by the old Ephraimite's daughter.

14. Joel 2:28; I have added the parts in brackets.

15. Kathleen Fischer, *Transforming Fire* (New York/ Mahwah, N. J.: Paulist Press, 1999), 131–32.

16. See Genesis, chapter 34.

17. See Genesis, chapter 16, and 21:1–21.

18. See 2 Samuel 13:1–22. The aftermath is told in 2 Samuel 13:23–14:27.

19. Esther 1:10. See chapter 1 of Esther for Queen Vashti's story.

20. Esther 1:22.

21. See Judges, chapter 11, especially 11:29–40. Note that she is given no name.

22. See Genesis 19:1–11.

"And they recognized him."

23. Phyllis Trible, *Texts of Terror: Literary-Feminist Readings of Biblical Narratives* (Philadelphia: Fortress Press, 1984), p. 81.

24. This was copyrighted in 1990 by the New York State Office for the Prevention of Domestic Violence, as adapted from the Domestic Abuse Intervention Project in Duluth, Minn.

25. According to *Violence in the Family: A Workshop Curriculum for Clergy and Other Helpers* by Marie M. Fortune (Cleveland: Pilgrim Press, 1991), © The Center for the Prevention of Sexual and Domestic Violence, Seattle, Washington, "95 percent of the victims of domestic violence are women."

26. See Gina Hens-Piazza, "Violence in Joshua and Judges," *The Bible Today*, July/August 2001 (Collegeville, Minn.: Liturgical Press), 197–203.

27. See Colossians 3:18–4:1 and Ephesians 5:21–6:9. These are Roman household codes which have been reframed into the context of Christ.

28. Hens-Piazza, p. 202. Phyllis Trible argues for a similar stance, saying that we need to repent of violence in our own lives.

29. Ibid.

30. Judges 19:1. Her story occupies the remainder of chapter 19, but the aftermath continues until the end of the book.

31. Judges 17:6 and 21:25, the very last verse of the book of Judges.

32. Judges 19:1. The use of the word concubine is unclear. She is very likely a "second wife," which would have been a common practice in those days, for reference is made to the Levite's father-in-law.

33. Trible, p. 66.

34. Judges 19:3.

35. See Hosea 2:14.

36. Judges 19:12.

37. Judges 19:22.

38. Judges 19:28.

39. Judges 19:29. Compare to Genesis 22:10, and the story of Abraham's "sacrifice" of Isaac.

40. Judges 19:29.

41. Trible, p. 64.

42. Isaiah 53:7, from the fourth Suffering Servant song; Christians later applied this to Jesus.

43. Judges 20:1, 3.

44. Judges 20:6.

45. Trible, p. 82; my emphasis.

46. Judges 20:13.

47. Judges 21:12.

48. Johanna Stiebert and Jerome T. Walsh, "Chaos Cries for a King," *The Bible Today*, July/August 2001 (Collegeville, Minn.: Liturgical Press), 215.

49. See 1 Samuel 1:9–11.

50. In the Babylonian Talmud she is credited with introducing prayer of petition, debating and pleading with God, like Moses, in the place of worship. She is also credited with calling God "Lord of Hosts" (*Zeva'ot*).

51. Hosea 9:9; see also Hosea 10:9.

52. Judges 19:30.

eight

CATHERINE OF SIENA

"The Fire of Our Love Is for Others"

....

Prayer Service Inspired by
St. Catherine of Siena

• •

FEAST DAY: APRIL 29

This prayer service is meant to be a pilgrimage prayer, a prayer of people joining with the fiery spirit of Catherine of Siena to seek the face of God. The pilgrimage leader (leader of prayer) will invite us into fourteenth-century Siena, where Catherine will join us as preacher. As people gather, there is candlelight throughout the worship space, giving a soft glow. There is just enough other light so that people feel at home. Light was essential to Catherine—it was the way of the "Sweet First Truth," one of her names for God and Christ. A Bridge of Passionate Love—central to Catherine's imaging of Christ—is the focal point of the worship space. (This could be a large picture on cardboard of a bridge made up of many kinds of stones.) In front of the bridge is a large basket with a variety of stones. Musicians are located on one side of the bridge, and the lectern and scripture on the other, with a candle stand nearby.

Before the service begins, people gather just outside the worship space, in a gathering area, if possible. Greeters welcome everyone and distribute the prayer programs. When it is time to begin, bells begin to peal, to proclaim the arrival of another day. The pilgrimage leader briefly welcomes everyone to fourteenth-century Siena and the journey into the heart of God. Little by little the light comes up, and the procession of pilgrims begins, led by Catherine carrying a large candle (to be placed on the candle stand next to the lectern), musicians (who begin the processional hymn), the lector, and the pilgrimage leader. The assembly of pilgrims follows.

Ministers: *pilgrimage leader, Catherine, musicians*

Materials: *Bridge of Passionate Love (picture), large basket of stones, lectern, scripture, candle stand, programs, bells*

Gathering Rites

· ·

PROCESSIONAL HYMN
· · · · · · · · · · · · · · · · ·

"As a Fire Is Meant for Burning," text by Ruth Duck, © 1992, GIA Publications, Inc., to the tune BEACH SPRING, *The Sacred Harp*, 1844, harm. by Marty Haugen, © 1985, GIA Publications, Inc.

CALL TO WORSHIP
· · · · · · · · · · · · · · ·

SUNG REFRAIN
· · · · · · · · · · · · ·

"Blest Are Those Who Love You," based on Psalm 128, a pilgrimage psalm, text and tune by Marty Haugen, © 1987, GIA Publications, Inc., refrain only, *led by the cantor; music continues softly under the leader and all parts.*

Leader: My soul waits for [our God],
          more than those who watch for the morning.[1]

All: And behold! Morning curtsies,
          radiant with the face of our God.

Leader: Listen! The Mangio, our slender, stately bell tower
          bids us begin another day.

"Were not our hearts burning within us?"

All: I lift up my eyes to the hills—
            from where will my help come?[2]

Leader: [Our] help comes from [God],[3]
            Who made heaven and earth.

All: We come, like Catherine before us,
            lifting up our eyes to the three hills of beloved Siena,
            creating that chapel deep within that is God's alone.

Leader: A pilgrimage leads from inside out,
            driven out into the street, like Catherine,
            to become another Christ.

All: Enter the hospital, home to plague victims in 1374.
            Hear the anguished cries for reconciliation rise up
            from the magnificent marbled black and white Duomo
            and the splendid center of public life, the Piazza del
            Campo.

Leader: Come, bless our God, all you seekers;
            lift up your hands to the holy place
            and bless our God.[4]

CANTOR AND ALL
. . . .

"Blest Are Those Who Love You," *refrain only, as before.*

OPENING PRAYER
. . . .

Leader: O Summoning, Seeking God,
            in the fullness of time You sent us your Word,
            fully clothed in the fabric of humanity, and the fire of
            your Love, to bridge the divide of human suffering.

All: Vest us, this day, with your burning zeal,
            that we might shed your light on darkened paths,
            and lift the chill from broken hearts.
            We pray this in the name of Jesus, the Christ. Amen.

"Were not our hearts burning within us?"

Catherine of Siena

Liturgy of the Word

READING: 1 JOHN 4:7–12

GOSPEL ALLELUIA

Alleluia refrain of Marty Haugen's "Easter Alleluia," or Alleluia from David Haas' *Mass of Light*, or Alleluia from Marty Haugen's *Mass of Remembrance*, all from GIA Publications, Inc. *During the Alleluia, Catherine comes forward, dressed in fourteenth-century clothing. She proclaims the gospel and preaches.*

GOSPEL: JOHN 3:16

HOMILY: "THE BRIDGE OF BLAZING LIFE"

Companions on the journey! *Welcome* to our pilgrimage here in Siena! We have crossed many a bridge to get here today, haven't we? The span of centuries. The divide of different cultures, perspectives, and tongues. In my day, church was the center of our lives. We had a devotion to the crucified Christ and would gaze upon the consecrated host. Penance was preached *everywhere,* and anyone who responded was held in high esteem. Many people— and most women—went without a formal education.

And yet, here we are, breathing in the same air. Taking in the same sweet goodness of God. And wrestling with some of the same troubles. Church is still divided and in need of reform. Political life is still riddled with squabbles. Families are still pulled apart over everyday matters, and women are still often regarded as less than men. Sickness still strikes with unexpected swiftness. People still lose a loved one and live with deep disappointments. But more than all that, the mystery of God profoundly continues to draw us, to warm us, to enflame our hearts with the passion of Christ, to move us across yet one more bridge, right here and right now.

I know how that feels. Don't you? What brings you here today? A gentle disturbance, like a job that no longer works or a gift that suddenly emerges? An inner gnawing or a tiny whisper (*Softly*)

"Were not our hearts burning within us?"

"There's more to life than this"? Or is it more like a strong driving wind, shattering everything in its wake? So much so that you might even feel like you're drowning! And you know, beyond any doubt, if not for God, "the flood would have swept [you] away, the torrent would have gone over [you]."[5] You find yourself asking, "Where am I? Who am I? Where is *God*? Which way do I go?"

And then you notice the bridge. It's a *beautiful* bridge, strong and imposing, made of stone, all kinds of stones. Yet it is strangely vulnerable and transparent to all who pass this way. You come closer, intrigued, drawn, almost as though the stones are calling out to you. Why, *this* stone is so inviting, with all its rough edges worn smooth. It speaks of welcome, healing, reviving, and restoring. And *this* one has marks embedded in it, like tear-drops. At its touch a surge of compassion wells up in you. Your hand reaches up to yet another stone, one that is slender and slightly curved, like an eagle in flight. What freedom you feel at its touch!

Are you surprised by the bridge, by what you see and feel? Perhaps the real surprise is this: the bridge is none other than Christ! Raised up by God, for us! On fire with love, for us! Yes, Christ is the only one capable of bridging the chasm of our no's and not yet's with the everlasting yes of God! What, then, are these stones? Why, they are "the virtues Christ practiced in his lifetime," held together by "the mortar of charity,"[6] the "blazing furnace of charity."[7]

Now you hear the call to follow. *Now* you see an unmistakable path on this bridge, with three stairs. Each one, considerably higher than the other. The path looks hard, you say. And so it is, for genuine love does not come easily. It burns away pretenses, and illusions. To forge what is most real, the intense love of God, for all. Listen to God's words of assurance about this bridge. It "is held together by my power and my Son's wisdom and the mercy of the Holy Spirit. My power gives the virtue of courage to those who follow this way. Wisdom gives them light to know the truth along the way. And the Holy Spirit gives them a love that uproots all"[8] selfish love, leaving only genuine love.

So you set out. Intent on taking that first step "with both feet— that is, with affection and desire."[9] You have three companions: the memory of God's blessings, understanding to reflect on such goodness, and a will to continue the journey. To get to the second step, you must choose to love what God loves, with your own free will. And when you do, "you come to the open side of God's Son. There you will find the fiery abyss of divine charity,"[10] that is the heart of Jesus. Such burning love propels you to the third and final step, the mouth of Christ. This is nothing less than union with Christ. Nothing less than a deep desire to serve Christ through our neighbor.

For me, this meant running lightly across the bridge whenever and wherever God called. Sometimes the call came to settle feuds between Siena and Florence, or between Florence and the Pope. And most assuredly, to plead with Pope Gregory XI in Avignon, for his return to Rome that the Church might be one. In fact, in all this, *nothing* could disturb the peace I felt. Not my sisters among the lay Dominicans who wanted to restrain me. Not the people who claimed my prayer was too passionate. Not the politicians who wanted conflict between the pope and the city of Florence. Nothing.

Companions on the journey, we are meant to become Christ's Body in *our* day. For God assured me, "I have set you as workers in your own and your neighbors' souls and in the mystic body of holy Church. In yourselves you must work at virtue; in your neighbors and in the Church you must work by example and teaching."[11] Praying for one another. Healing. Forgiving. And restoring one another. Yes, my friends, we *must* become a bridge of burning love for one another. We *must* become another Christ.

MUSICAL REFLECTION
. . . .

"For the Healing of the Nations," text is the eleventh century *Angularis fundamentum*, translated by John M. Neale, tune is St. Thomas.

Silence

"Were not our hearts burning within us?"

Ritual of Building the Bridge of Love

INTRODUCTION (The Pilgrimage Leader)

The Bridge of Christ is a sacred place. The place where steadfast love and faithfulness meet, where righteousness and peace embrace.[12] It is the place where the demon of silence in the face of fear is expelled. A place where the demon of illusion is stripped away, so that truth may be revealed. It is the place where selfishness gives way to genuine love. The bridge of Christ's Body is made up of many living stones or virtues: wisdom, courage, prophesy, servant leadership, compassion, patience, understanding, creativity, and passionate love, among others. Catherine will now lead us in blessing these virtues, or "living stones."

Music (not yet words) of "Song Over the Waters" begins and continues softly during the blessing.

BLESSING OF THE STONES

Catherine: Listen deeply to the stillness of your soul.
Listen, where the stones of Christ's bridge will speak.

All: We will listen to the landscape of our souls.

Catherine: Your soul knows well the virtues that God has placed there, waiting to be discovered, explored, and developed.

All: We will wait, until we recognize our special virtues.

Catherine
and all: Christ, Sweet First Truth,
Inflame us with understanding and truth,
that these precious stones, our virtues,
will become building blocks of Your bridge,
for healing, reviving, and restoring our world. Amen.

Invitation by the pilgrimage leader to choose a Living Stone:

Leader: Please come forward and take a stone from the basket.

Catherine of Siena

Allow it to become a Living Stone, a source of prayer now and in the days ahead. Allow it to help you recognize your special virtue in the building of Christ's bridge. Then please go to one of our leaders, who will ask, "Who are you?" You can answer, in truth, "I am a Living Stone" or "I am a Living Stone of _____." She will then bless you in this desire.

MUSIC
· · · · ·

"Song Over the Waters," text and tune by Marty Haugen, © 1987, GIA Publications, Inc.

Closing Rites
· ·

The lights go down and the bells resume, signaling the close of another day. The pilgrimage leader returns.

PILGRIMAGE LEADER
· · · · · · · · · · · · · · · · · · · ·

It is the end of another day on our journey. And the bells of the Mangio might well have tolled like this on April 29 in the year of our Lord 1380, to mark the end of Catherine's scant thirty-three years on this earth. But, Catherine, your spirit is with us forever. We know you as teacher, as Doctor of the Church, and as a lay Dominican. We know you as mystic, as spouse of Christ, as woman passionately in love with your Sweet First Truth. We know you as courageous minister to victims of the plague in 1374 and as diplomat, as ambassador for Christ to warring factions of your day. We know you as powerful preacher and writer of letters . . . to people "high" and "low." We know you as faithful woman, yet tempted at the end of your life to doubt the meaning of all you had done. We know that the church unity you poured out your life for would take another stubborn thirty-five years to achieve, that your cherished dream of a "papal council" of holy men and women came to nothing, and that the community of followers you left behind in Siena would fall apart. But most of all, we know you as a woman of passion, on fire for God and the Christ hidden in

"Were not our hearts burning within us?"

every human face, staking your life on the truth that what matters in life is love alone, staking your life on justice that is clothed in the garment of love. As we leave you today, Catherine, would you bless us on our way?

BLESSING

. . . .

Invite each half of the room to face one another and extend an arm in blessing as Catherine proclaims:

Catherine: Friends of Sweet First Truth, may you be made holy in the truth, which is God alone,

All: Amen.

Catherine: And may you rest secure in the sea of God's love,

All: Amen.

Catherine: So that together you may become the Living Body of Christ, the bridge, providing healing, reconciliation and nourishment to our broken world.

All: Amen.

CLOSING HYMN

. . . .

"Easter Alleluia," ancient hymn tune, O FILII ET FILIAE, adapted by Marty Haugen, © 1986, GIA Publications, Inc.

An Interview with Catherine of Siena

. . . .

Interviewer: Hello, everyone! Welcome! Today we are privileged to have with us a woman of fourteenth-century Europe, Catherine of Siena. She is a woman of contradictions. A frail woman, yet one of gigantic stature. A young virgin who clothed herself—at age eighteen— in the Dominican habit of lay widows, the mantellate.[13] A woman of prayer who cloistered herself at home for nearly three years, only to be pushed by the Holy Spirit out into the streets of her beloved Siena, ministering to the poor and the sick, the leprous and the plague victims, touching the ones nobody else wanted to touch.[14] A woman of intense reverence for God who dared to chastise God for sending her, a woman, into the halls of political and ecclesial power. As she put it, "My very sex, as I need not tell you, puts many obstacles in the way. The world has no use of women in work such as that, and propriety forbids a woman to mix so freely in the company of men."[15] A woman of spirit, of intense personal warmth and charm, who never hesitated to bluntly speak her truth of God to anyone who needed to hear it, even two popes. A woman who lived only thirty-three years but whose shadow looms large over the church. A woman who was never formally educated but who is responsible for a Dialogue with God the Father, twenty-six prayers recorded by her disciples, and 381 letters addressed to popes and royalty, artisans, and family members.[16] Indeed, she is only the second woman named a Doctor of the Church . . . on October 4, 1970, by Pope Paul VI.[17] Catherine, you have traveled across time and space to be with us today. Thank you! Would you begin by telling us about your hometown of Siena? What was it like in your lifetime, 1347 to 1380?

Catherine: Of course! What a beautiful city, my beloved Siena! From the valley below, you look up and see the burnt orange town, perched on the crest of our three hills. As you make your way through the gate, you come upon a place that was home to me, the church of San Domenico. It is simple, yet stately and sturdy . . . large, yet welcoming to all. Once inside, I still hear the echoes of so many powerful Dominican sermons. Clarion calls to penance and contrition for our sins. Urgent messages to weep at turning away from God. And gospel challenges . . . in the tradition of St. Augustine . . . to ignite the sparks of God's Love within us. How? Through the memory of God's goodness, blazing for us from the cross. Through the light of our understanding. And through the will to desire what God desires. But now, come, you must see the pride and joy of so many in Siena. The center of city life, the Piazza del Campo, the place of our public market. Follow me, as we wend our way through some of the narrow city streets, until . . . our breath is taken away! Suddenly we emerge onto a vast space, spreading out, like a fan, before us. Our eyes take in the feast, drawn first to the majestic Palazzo Pubblico, home of the Ruling Nine. Then, to the bell tower, the tall, slender, stately Torre della Mangia, nestled next to the Palazzo. It is the pealing of these bells that sounds the beginning and end of every day. Completed in 1347, the year of my birth, it is the boast of Siena. But, as I look out onto this magnificent space, I can only see the shape of the Virgin Mary's veil, protecting our city from harm.

We go further up, through some of the oldest parts of the city, to the highest point in town. The magnificent Duomo, striped in black and white marble, a church to compete with the cathedral of Florence. Immediately across the way is the hospital, home to so many victims of the plague, home to those who cry out for gospel healing, home to my first ministry outside my immediate family.

Siena is alive and changing. It is a city of families—I was the second youngest of twenty-five Benincasa children, myself. It is a city where families know one another, where people have their place but where place can change. My own father, Giacomo Benincasa, was a relatively prosperous dye-maker, and we lived in an area below the nobles but above the artisans and peasants. He was even able to serve in the popolo, led by the Ruling Nine. Trade was changing the way people did business, but it could not stop the tragedy of the plague. The church was in a time of upheaval as well, in need of much reform. But more on that, later.

Interviewer: Yes, Catherine, I do want to get to that. But, first, would you tell us how you came to know God and how God laid a claim on your life?

Catherine: I will never forget that day, even though I was only six years old. For on that day, I was on my way home from visiting one of my married sisters, and I was given a beautiful vision: the Lord Jesus sitting on a throne, clad in pontifical robes, looking at me with such tender love and blessing me. Next to him were the apostles Peter, Paul, and John. Little did I know, then, how important they would be in my life! The next year, even though I was only seven, I vowed to serve God in perpetual virginity, and I knew what that meant. But, as a young teenager, I seemed to forget that pledge for awhile, giving in to the desires of my family to look pleasing to a man. Then came my moment of decision. When I was fifteen, my beloved sister, Bonaventura, died in childbirth. I came to my senses! And I renewed my vow, my energy, and my commitment to serve God above all else. My family fiercely resisted; they kept me busy with household chores and even eliminated my prayer space. As it turned out, this was a blessing. For I discovered a cell, a home for God, deep within myself. Finally, when my father saw the depth of my determination, he insisted that my whole family support me in my vocation. And one year later I embraced the mission of the mantellate, living in prayerful seclusion at home for the next three years.

Interviewer: Catherine, you are a woman of passion! Your desire, your burning love for God are revealed in that tender name for God, "Sweet First Truth." Would you tell us about the development of this relationship?

Catherine: You are right, there is a burning passion inside me, to "give myself completely to seeking God's honor, the salvation of souls, and the renewal and exaltation of holy church."[18] My relationship with God is not just for me, but for the good of others. How certain I was of this when I had a vision of streams of people entering the side of Christ crucified![19] So, you must understand; I do not speak of this relationship as a personal possession.

Interviewer: Yes, I appreciate your humility and your dedication. And so many people today desire a deeper relationship with God, struggling to integrate this relationship into an active life, as you did. Whatever you can offer us in this regard would be so helpful.

Catherine: Yes, of course, I do see that. What can I say, except that in prayer I came to know myself in God and God in myself? I came to see that God's heart is such a "deep well of charity," that God is so "madly in love" with us that he cannot seem to live without us.[20] I came to know God as the "One who is" and myself as the "one who is not."[21] But this only deepened my love, for I came to see "that through no merit" of my own, but by God's creation, I am—we all are—"the image of God."[22] What a passion has been kindled in me! "In your nature, eternal Godhead, I shall come to know my nature. And what is my nature, boundless love? It is fire, because you are nothing but a fire of love. And . . . by the fire of love you created us."[23] Yes, God is like a mother who feeds us with the milk of real presence, only to create in us a thirst for God's every desire.[24] God is the love who strengthens us in trials, who so expands our hearts that there is room for nothing—in the end—but compassion . . . and zeal for the healing of this broken world that God is so passionately in love with.

And for me, God is none other than truth, that which is most real.[25] Truth was there in the beginning, in love, calling forth, forming, and shaping all of creation. Truth has been there ever since, a saving truth, calling each and every person to see and to follow what is most real, stripping away all illusions of what pretends to be real. There is pain and struggle in all this, but the sea of God's mercy for us is beyond all imagining. For truth is always a lover, desiring oneness with each and every human heart. Yes, truth is at the heart of the world.

Interviewer: And how do you envision Christ?

Catherine: Christ is also my "Sweet First Truth," for as God declared to me, "I, the invisible, made myself visible as it were in the Word, my only-begotten Son."[26] He is "my truth," my plan that people be "united to me by love."[27] Christ crucified, in whose name I wrote so many letters, is the revealer of God's foolish love for each and every one of us, for there was no "nail sufficient to keep him fixed and nailed to the cross," only "his ineffable love for our salvation."[28] On his cross, he became our teacher, wisdom enthroned for all to see.

Christ is also the way to the truth, a bridge of living stones. For Christ is the choice to love. The only bridge capable of spanning the abyss of human disobedience. As God explained to me, "The stones of the virtues are built on him by my power, since there is not a single virtue which has not been tested in him, and by him all are made alive. Therefore, nobody can have any virtue that gives the life of grace, except from him, by following him and his doctrine closely. He has matured all virtues and set them, like living stones held together with his blood, so that everyone may go speedily and without fear."[29] The first step onto this bridge is taken at the feet of Christ, nailed to the cross. This step is still mixed with selfish interests and fear. The second step is the hardest. The difficult trek to the entrance of his heart, through the wound of his side. This step requires daily practice in prayer and virtue, tested in the decisions to love our neighbors. Finally, we are brought to that perfect love of union, where we are embraced by the mouth of Christ. Why? To become another Christ in the world, acting and speaking on Christ's behalf.

Interviewer: Your age was filled with tensions: political upheavals, church upheavals, nation-states flexing their new muscles, vying for power with the papacy, even keeping the pope under French control in Avignon for much of the fourteenth century. There were political rivalries and squabbles among city-states, like that between Siena and Florence. There was obvious need for reform in much of the church. Since we have so many struggles today, in church and society, could you comment on your own?

Catherine: You have said it well; it was a time of painful division, in so many ways. And I endured the brunt of that division in my very being because I was a woman, a diplomat, and a seeker after church reform. Let me explain. There were critics, early on, who ridiculed my ministry in the streets, just because I was a woman. And I even complained to God, for sending a woman into the thick of all these conflicts.

But the word of God was swift and sure in response, "Does it not depend on my own will where I shall pour out my grace? With me there is no longer male and female, nor lower and upper class; for all stand equal in my sight."[30] Indeed, my confessor and very dear friend, Raymond of Capua, insisted that he could see the hand of God at work in all this. As he put it, just as God sent unschooled apostles to confound the arrogance of the educated leaders in their day, so God continues to send "women filled with the power and wisdom of God" to church leaders. Indeed, if men listen humbly, "welcoming and heeding, with all due submission," to the women God sends them, divine mercy will be poured out on the church.[31]

Then, of course, there were the political leaders who called on me to help reconcile conflicts. And yet, soon after I responded, some of them turned on me, accusing me of plotting against them. Right here in Siena! And in Florence, too, where I was nearly killed for trying to heal the rift between Florentine leaders and the pope.

But, the source of my deepest agony was the schism in the church, which is meant to be a place of God's nourishment for all people. Yes, I reserved my harshest words of truth for three cardinals. The three who had spearheaded the election of Clement VII, a second pope, in opposition to Pope Urban VI. "Had you seen it," I wrote, "you would not have deserted the truth so lightly in servile fear. What made you do this?" Only the "poison" of selfishness, I concluded.[32]

Interviewer: Yes, Catherine, despite all your trials, you were not afraid to immerse yourself in the midst of all this strife. Somehow, you managed to integrate an active life, filled with stress, into your intense prayer life. Your words of wisdom on all this will be welcomed by many of us today.

Catherine: The ultimate point, for me, is that love is at the heart of the universe. And I must be so in touch with that truth that it becomes my very own. For the truth of God is always a saving truth, a healing truth. It means passionately entering into the concrete pain of our brothers and sisters so as to heal that pain. What wars against doing such truth? Selfishness and fear. And silence born of this fear, for "it is silence which kills the world."[33] What empowers us to act boldly, even in the midst of tension and strife? Only the love of God that enfolds the universe, the sea of love that is the triune God. And the growing realization, washing over us in that love, that anything outside of God's truth is only an illusion of power. Think about Pentecost. Think about the cowardice and fear of many of Jesus' first disciples during the passion; and think about their powerful transformation as the Spirit of truth and love hovered over them. At that moment, "through love they lost their fear,"[34] for "perfect love casts out fear," as it says in 1 John 4:18. That same love, that same power is available to each and every one of us, for God is continually wooing each of us to become a "spouse of the truth."[35] All we need do is to pray as I did, "Clothe, clothe me with yourself, Eternal Truth."[36] And God will quickly respond, with clothing that is woven from the very fiber of our own experience.

Interviewer: It has been said, Catherine, that even on your deathbed you were tempted to doubt all that you had done for

WALKING WITH WISDOM'S DAUGHTERS

"Were not our hearts burning within us?"

the life of the church. Would you be willing to comment on this?

Catherine: It's true! I had poured out my life, fasted and prayed, acted with the passion of Jesus, for the sake of the church I loved so much, to bring us together as one. But failure followed upon failure! Yes, Pope Gregory XI had finally returned from Avignon in 1377, three years before my death. But, then, his successor, Pope Urban VI, became a tyrant! He was roundly rejected by half of Christendom! A second so-called Pope, Clement VII, was chosen.[37]

As if that wasn't enough, my dearest friend, Raymond of Capua, left Rome late in 1378 to become papal legate to King Charles V, and we would never see each other again. Not only that, Raymond backed out of a plan to preach a crusade against Clement, fearful because of almost certain assassination. Indeed, I felt responsible for his cowardice and wrote him, "Am I always, because of my faithlessness, to shut the gates against Divine Providence?"[38] Even my cherished dream of a "papal council" of holy men and women came to nothing.

Finally, as I became weaker and weaker in those last two months from the offering of my very self for the unity of the church, I began to hear that even my community of followers in Siena was falling apart. Had I utterly failed? But, then, I remembered Jesus. Would his life have been counted a "success" at the time of his death? Was success what he had come for? Of course not! He came to be faithful to God's way of love, even if it meant revealing the fire of that love from the height of the cross. It has always been true that we Christians have struggled with the "scandal" of the cross, hasn't it?

Interviewer: Catherine, what are your final words of wisdom to us?

Catherine: Only this, always this: The love of God is poured out for us all, the gentle love of my Sweet First Truth. Our call is to surrender to that merciful love, which is

"Were not our hearts burning within us?"

always like a sea of peace, regardless of what goes on around us. Our call is to faithfulness to that love, in good times and in bad. This alone makes possible the endurance of failure, misunderstanding, and even ridicule for the sake of this love. For, indeed, love is the only measure of a life well lived. Let me conclude with God's very own words, "I have put you among your neighbors so that you can do for them what you cannot do for me . . . love them without any concern for thanks and without looking for any profit for yourself. And whatever you do for them I will consider done for me."[39] That, dear friends, is the greatest gift I can offer you today.

SOME RESOURCES
· · · · · · · · · · · · · · ·

Catherine of Siena. *The Letters of Catherine of Siena*. Trans. Suzanne Noffke. Binghamton, New York, 1988.

Cavallini, Guiliana, OP. *Catherine of Siena*. London and New York: Geoffrey Chapman, 1998.

Fatula, Mary Ann, OP. *Catherine of Siena's Way*. Wilmington, Del.: Michael Glazier, Inc., 1987, revised 1990 and published in Collegeville, Minnesota, Michael Glazier Books.

Meade, Catherine M., CSJ. *My Nature Is Fire*. New York: Alba House, 1991.

Noffke, Suzanne, OP, trans. and introduction. *Catherine of Siena: The Dialogue*. New York: Paulist Press, 1980.

_____. *The Prayers of Catherine of Siena*. New York: Paulist Press, 1983.

_____. *Catherine of Siena: Vision Through a Distant Eye*. Collegeville, Minn.: A Michael Glazier Book, 1996.

NOTES
· · · · ·

1. Taken from Psalm 130:6, another pilgrimage psalm.

2. Taken from Psalm 121:1, another pilgrimage psalm.

3. Taken from Psalm 121:2.

4. Adapted from Psalm 134:1–2, the last of the pilgrimage psalms.

5. See Psalm 124:4.

WALKING WITH WISDOM'S DAUGHTERS

"Were not our hearts burning within us?"

6. Guiliana Cavallini, OP, *Catherine of Siena* (London and New York: Geoffrey Chapman, 1998), 71–72.

7. Catherine M. Meade, CSJ, *My Nature Is Fire* (New York: Alba House, 1991), 167.

8. Suzanne Noffke, OP, translator, *Catherine of Siena: The Dialogue* (New York: Paulist Press, 1980), 70.

9. Meade, p. 110, quoting from *The Dialogue* of Catherine, 49: 100–101.

10. Meade, p. 111, quoting from Catherine's *Letters*, 62, p. 198.

11. Noffke, p. 159.

12. See Psalm 85:10.

13. The *mantellate*, named after the black veil they wore over the white Dominican habit, dated back to the thirteenth century, the time of Dominic. The first *mantellate* were widows of laymen who had formed the Militia of Jesus Christ, renamed The Brothers of Penance of St. Dominic. Other widows began to join these Sisters of Penance of St. Dominic; Catherine was the first virgin to do so. They lived in their own homes and devoted themselves to prayer and care of the sick.

14. There were two bouts with the plague in Siena during Catherine's lifetime; the first was in 1348, the year after her birth and the second was in 1374. During the first, the population of Siena was cut in half.

15. Mary Ann Fatula, OP, *Catherine of Siena's Way* (Wilmington, Del.: Michael Glazier, 1987, 1990), 42–43.

16. The *Letters* were dictated to her secretaries and date from 1370 to 1380. Her *Prayers* were simply recorded by some of her disciples as she prayed; some go back to her time in Avignon, but most date from her time in Rome, December 1378 to spring 1380. Catherine dictated her *Dialogue* between the autumn of 1377 and October 1378; this last is the story of humanity itself, as well as the story of one woman, Catherine, seeking perfection. The creature, touched by God, longs with all that is in her to know the truth of God and herself.

17. Teresa of Avila was the first woman so named, only a few days earlier, on September 29, 1970.

18. *Letters*, p. 208, as found in Meade, p 87.

19. Letter to Raymond of Capua and some followers as found in Meade, p. 86. Catherine was twenty-nine years old at the time.

20. Catherine's *Dialogue* 25, p. 63, as found in Fatula, p. 145.

21. *Prayers* 11:95 and 14:123, as found in Meade, p. 92.

22. Catherine's *Dialogue* 13:41, as found in Meade, p. 91.

23. *Prayers*, 12, p. 104, as found in Fatula, p. 171.

24. Fatula, p. 92.

25. Catherine was a lay Dominican and might well have been influenced by the motto of the Dominican order, *Veritas*, meaning Truth.

26. Catherine's *Dialogue* LXII, as found in Cavallini, p. 68.

27. Catherine's *Dialogue* I, as found in Cavallini, p. 68; at several points in the *Dialogue* Catherine referred to Christ as "my Truth."

28. Letter 102, as found in Cavallini, p. 71.

29. Catherine's *Dialogue* XXVII, as found in Cavallini, pp. 71–72.

30. Raymond of Capua, *The Life of Catherine of Siena*, translated and annotated by Conleath Kearns, OP (Wilmington, Del.: Michael Glazier, Inc., 1980), 116–17, as quoted in Fatula, pp. 42–43.

31. Ibid.

32. *Letter T*, 296, to three Italian cardinals, in *St. Catherine of Siena as Seen in Her Letters*, translated and edited with Introduction by Vida D. Scudder (New York: E.P. Dutton 1927), 281, 278, as found in Fatula, p. 64.

33. *Letter T*, 16, to a prelate, as found in Fatula, p. 72.

34. *Letter T*, 94, to Frate Matteo di Francesco Tolomei, OP, in Scudder, p. 87, as found in Fatula, p. 71.

35. Fatula, p. 71.

36. The closing prayer of her *Dialogue*, 167, p. 377, as found in Fatula, p. 75.

37. By 1379, the Christian world was torn in two. Central Italy, Venice, Milan, Genoa, Flanders, and England supported Urban VI. Savoy, Naples, Spain, Avignon, Scotland, and France followed Clement VII. Unity was not restored until the Council of Constance (1414–18) and the election of Martin V as pope in 1417.

38. *Letter T*, 344, to Raymond of Capua, as found in Fatula, p. 37.

39. Catherine's *Dialogue*, 64, p. 121, as found in Fatula, pp. 138–39.

"Were not our hearts burning within us?"

nine

"Woman Caught

in Adultery"

Repentance and Forgiveness of Sins Is to Be Proclaimed to All

....

We Are Witnesses to This Message

....

Greeters offer a program to people as they enter and invite them to select a stone—whatever appeals—from a nearby basket. Chairs are best placed in a semi-circle, and the focal point is in the center of the gathering. It is a table that displays a wilderness scene (possibly with some sand and a cactus). On this table there is also a basket that will be used during the ritual to deposit the stones. There is enough room for people to "enact" the gospel story, complete with the narrator, Jesus, the woman, the temple police, the scribes, and the Pharisees. Musicians and cantor gather at one end of the semi-circle; lector, the woman, and the prayer leader are seated at the other. Jesus, the narrator, the temple police, and the Pharisees speak from the assembly.

Ministers: prayer leader, greeters, narrator, Jesus, the woman, the temple police, Nicodemus, two scribes, two Pharisees, musicians, cantor, lector

Materials: *programs, stones, two baskets, chairs, table, wilderness scene*
(such as sand and cactus)

Gathering Rites

••

CALL TO WORSHIP
• • • • • • • • • • • • • • •

Leader: Stones can be projectiles of punishment . . .
            hard-heartedness in motion . . .

All: Jagged missiles propelled at adulterers . . .
            and others, intended to control, maim, isolate, and
            destroy.

Leader: But there is one who is a Living Stone,
            cornerstone of a people built on mercy,

All: Compassion poured out, healing justice.

Leader: Come to Christ, then, "a living stone,
            though rejected by mortals
            yet chosen and precious in God's sight. . ."[1]

All: Like "living stones,"
            build us, O Christ, into "a holy priesthood,"[2]
            a balm of justice for our world. Amen.

OPENING HYMN
• • • • • • • • • • • • • •

"Healer of Our Every Ill," text and tune by Marty Haugen, ©
1987, GIA Publications, Inc.

Liturgy of the Word

••

FIRST READING: ISAIAH 43:16–21
• •

PSALM 126
• • • • • • • •

"God Has Done Great Things for Us," text and tune by Marty
Haugen, © 1988, GIA Publications, Inc.

GOSPEL ACCLAMATION

. . . .

"Glory to you, O Word of God, Lord Jesus Christ," music from the *Mass of Light* by David Haas, © 1988, GIA Publications, Inc.

GOSPEL: JOHN 7:32B, 45–48, 7:50–8:11

. . . .

Told in word and action by the narrator, Jesus, the woman, the temple police, Nicodemus, scribes, and Pharisees. Words in italics, spoken by the leader, are not part of scripture.

Leader: *This story takes place in the fall of the year, during the Feast of Booths in Jerusalem. It is a seven-day harvest feast, when many pilgrims come to the Temple. Now, at this time, the Pharisees heard that many in the crowd believed in Jesus.*

Narrator: The chief priests and Pharisees sent temple police to arrest him . . .

Then the temple police went back to the chief priests and Pharisees, who asked them,

Scribes &
Pharisees: "Why did you not arrest him?

Police: "Never has anyone spoken like this!"

Pharisees: "Surely you have not been deceived too, have you? Has any one of the authorities or of the Pharisees believed in him?"

Narrator: Nicodemus, who had gone to Jesus before, and who was one of them, asked,

Nicodemus: "Our law does not judge people without first giving them a hearing to find out what they are doing, does it?"

Pharisees: "Surely you are not also from Galilee, are you? Search and you will see that no prophet is to arise from Galilee."

"Woman Caught in Adultery"   159

Narrator: Then each of them went home, while Jesus went to the Mount of Olives. Early in the morning he came again to the temple. All the people came to him and he sat down and began to teach them. The scribes and the Pharisees brought a woman who had been caught in adultery; and making her stand before all of them, they said to him,

Scribes &
Pharisees: "Teacher, this woman was caught in the very act of committing adultery. Now in the law Moses commanded us to stone such women. Now what do you say?"

Narrator: They said this to test him, so that they might have some charge to bring against him. Jesus bent down and wrote with his finger on the ground. When they kept on questioning him, he straightened up and said to them,

Jesus: "Let anyone among you who is without sin be the first to throw a stone at her."

Narrator: And once again he bent down and wrote on the ground. When they heard it, they went away, one by one, beginning with the elders; and Jesus was left alone with the woman standing before him. Jesus straightened up and said to her,

Jesus: "Woman, where are they? Has no one condemned you?"

Woman: "No one, sir."

Jesus: "Neither do I condemn you. Go your way, and from now on do not sin again."

Narrator: The Gospel of the Lord.

REFLECTION (The Woman)

● ● ● ● ● ● ● ● ● ● ● ● ● ● ● ● ● ● ●

Have you ever been stuck in life? Overwhelmed, with no way out? I have. I've even been caught in a barrage of hateful words. Poised, like so many missiles, for the kill.

But the miracle is the healing . . . the way through, the ability to speak, confidently, honestly, beyond fear of retribution. The ability to say no in peace. Without vengeance. Without the desire to hurt in return. "No, somebody else's idol will *not* control my life. Not any longer." How did that happen? Let me tell you about it.

Here I am, once again, on the Mount of Olives . . . delighting in the delicious breath of life. Oh, how I *love* to come here early in the morning, while it's still cool! Especially this time of the year . . . the fall . . . with the plump aroma of full-grown olives hanging in the air. Aaaahh! Can't you smell it? Can't you almost feel the penetrating warmth of its massaging oil? With the shadows lifting here at dawn, can't you see the Temple looming large over Jerusalem? Can't you almost see Jesus, once again, stepping onto the Temple precincts? Can't you almost hear him teaching fearlessly, one more time? Authentically, with words intended to pry open fisted hearts? Words that Jesus found right here, in prayer, on the Mount of Olives, whenever he needed them. God-given words. Heart-strength words.

Here, at dawn, it is hard for me to remember that there ever was a time when I lived in shadows, cowering under someone else's control. For that heart-strength of Jesus becomes mine, right here, right now. Even as I relive, once again, that day I'll *never* forget. Clamoring crowds surge toward me . . . pilgrims there for the Feast of Booths. Arrogant scribes and Pharisees shove me toward Jesus! And I am once again on trial! Or so I think. I'm condemned. Doomed. I know the law, and I'm liable to death under it. For we are taught that "if a man is caught lying with the wife of another man, both of them shall die, the man who lay with the woman as well as the woman."[3] And I know the reason for the law. The men need to preserve their honor and the purity of their male offspring. But, there's a lot I didn't know yet. That it's my very own husband who has set me up. Oh, I had felt his control, time and time again; it had even become bone of my bone and flesh of my flesh. But I couldn't imagine that he would stoop to this stripping of my dignity! He knew that I hungered for basic human affection, and he guessed that I would give myself to anyone who seemed to offer it. So, here I stand, with no way out, feeling utterly naked before eyes that are mocking me.

And then I begin to see. *I'm* not the one on trial. I'm just another object, once again . . . soon to become an object lesson. It's *Jesus* that the religious leaders are really after. *He's* the one to be condemned. For he has healed on the Sabbath. Why, there's even talk that he's the Messiah! No matter what he says, he's done for, or so they think. If he refuses to indict me, he will reject the law of Moses. If he calls for my stoning, he will break the new Roman law, forbidding the Sanhedrin to impose the death penalty. They're almost smacking their lips with certain victory! There's no way out for Jesus!

Until . . . Jesus draws a line in the sand with a few short words. Accountability, yes. Condemnation, no. Life beyond imagining, yes. Deadly control, no, whether at home or at the hands of religious authorities. Suddenly, *they* are the ones on trial. One by one, they silently slink away . . . having found *themselves* guilty. Even the crowd begins to thin out, until I am alone with the healing words of Jesus.

But healing is never once and for all. That's why I come here, so often, to the Mount of Olives. For peace . . . healing . . . and heart-strength. It's *here* that I remember Jesus. And know his presence. It's *here* that I feel safe. It's *here* that I begin to see the sin of domination, condemnation, and control. It's *here* that I can say no—one more time—to my part in that sin. No to passivity in the face of threat and domination. No to my too eager desire to please. No to my tendency to fall back into being the victim. No to my temptation to condemn in return. Only then can I pronounce my yes. Yes, to drawing my own line in the sand. Yes, to accountability. Yes, to Jesus, the cornerstone my life. Yes, to the gift of another new day!

Silence

MUSICAL RESPONSE
. . . .

"Loving Hands," text and tune by Cary Ratcliff, © 1991, Kairos Music Publishers, P.O. Box 10165, Rochester, NY 14610. *This is a beautiful hymn, which reflects upon this gospel story.*

Ritual of Reconciliation

INTERCESSIONS

Leader: We know well the many stones of human violence. Against us. Within us. Around us. We also know the Living Stone, who is Christ. The only one who can make a way where there is no way. The only one who can transform violence into compassion, sin into the possibility of new life. Therefore, we bring all our needs for healing . . . and beginning again . . . to Christ, our living stone.

MUSICAL RESPONSE TO EACH INTERCESSION

"In Love You Summon," using only the first part of the text: "In love you summon, in love I follow, living today for your tomorrow," text and tune by John Bell, © 1998, Iona Community. GIA Publications, Inc., exclusive North American agent.

INVITATION TO LAY DOWN OUR STONES OF SIN

Leader: We all carry the heavy burden of sin. Passivity. Self-righteousness. Blaming and condemning. We also know what it is to be on the receiving end of such sin. Even the eminent theologian, Yves Congar, one of the architects of the Second Vatican Council, was stripped of his dignity and silenced by leaders of the Church in the 1950s. He cried out in anguish, "I am crushed, destroyed, abused, disowned by all. I have to deal with a wicked system, a system incapable of correcting itself, that never recognizes its own injustices, that is served by men stripped of goodness and mercy."[4]

Take a moment, now, to reflect quietly, cradling your stone in your hand. How does this stone speak to you of your sinfulness? What must you lay down, along with this stone, to move along the path of radical newness? How can this stone then become a "living stone," a witness to Jesus, our cornerstone? What do you most need for that to happen?

The leader, narrator, woman, and Pharisee will model the following ritual for us. They will come forward to the basket and lay down their stone. Then, they will declare to one another (woman and Pharisee, narrator and leader) their desire to leave their sinfulness behind, so that they might become "living stones" of witness. As you are ready, you are invited to do the same. After you deposit your stone in the basket, you may go to one of the four leaders and say something like, "May God transform me into a living stone."

MUSIC DURING THE RITUAL

"Hosea," text based on Hosea and Joel, text and tune by Gregory Norbet, © 1972, 1980, The Benedictine Foundation of the State of Vt., Inc.

and

"You Are Mine," text and tune by David Haas, © 1991, GIA Publications, Inc.

Closing Rites

BLESSING/COMMISSIONING

Left and right "sides" face one another, with an arm extended in blessing.

Left: Hands are capable of violence,
            hot hatred in motion,
            battered become battering,
            stones frozen into "I don't care."

Right: But hands healed by compassion poured out,
            can become, instead,
            warmth for the weary,
            and justice for the thirsty.

All: Go forth, then, in Christ,
         Our Living Stone,
         mercy embraced by justice,
         source of balm for our world. Amen.

CLOSING HYMN (*sung as a round*)
· ·

"Behold, I Make All Things New," text and tune from the Iona Community, © 1995, Iona Community. GIA Publications, Inc., exclusive North American agent.

The "Woman Caught in Adultery" John 7:53–8:11

· ·

She has found a home in John's gospel, but scripture scholars are not sure where she belongs. (Perhaps she is symbolic of women in church in this regard.) It is agreed that the story of the "woman caught in adultery" is an authentic part of the Jesus tradition, for it is referenced in the third century Syrian *Didascalia Apostolorum* (*Teaching of the Apostles*). However, she is missing from the earliest Greek manuscripts of John's gospel. We do not find her in the standard Greek text until about 900, but Jerome includes her in his Latin Vulgate, early in the fifth century. Such inclusion, for Catholics, provides a strong argument for canonicity.

Her history gives rise to several questions. Why the delay in including her in scripture? And where does she really belong? With regard to the former, several explanations have been offered. But for Raymond Brown, the most plausible is the ease of Jesus in forgiving this woman, in marked contrast to the harsh system of public penance that developed in the early centuries of the Church.[5] With regard to the latter, some scholars, like Raymond Brown, find her stylistically compatible with Luke, rather than John.

Indeed, some suggest that she "belongs" after Luke 21:38, during Jesus' final days in Jerusalem; her story would then be immediately followed by the plot to kill Jesus. But, she could fit in either place, for, as Raymond Brown so succinctly puts it, this story of the compassion of Jesus "is as delicate as anything in Luke; its portrayal of Jesus as the serene judge has all the majesty that we would expect of John."[6] And theologically, she does, indeed, belong at the beginning of John's eighth chapter, woven from beginning to end with themes of judgment and truth.

This story is a trial scene. Clearly, the woman knows she is on trial. How she must have cringed, as men of authority hauled her before the judgment seat, in full view of the huge crowds gathered in the Temple precincts for the Feast of Booths. And the law of Moses is very clear. "If a man is caught lying with the wife of another man, both of them shall die, the man who lay with the woman as well as the woman. So you shall purge the evil from Israel" (Dt 22:22). The Book of Leviticus (20:10) reiterates this command. As far as the means of execution, stoning is suggested for a betrothed young woman, who has betrayed her beloved by sleeping with another man (Dt 22:21). Perhaps the most gruesome—even misogynist—account of punishment is to be found in the prophet Ezekiel (16:38–41), where a woman could be stripped and then stoned by a mob, and finally cut to "pieces with their swords."

As the story develops, however, it is clear that the religious leaders have really put Jesus on trial—or so they think. Many in the crowd of pilgrims have come to believe that he is the Messiah. And the Pharisees must put a stop to this! Here is the perfect trap; on one side is the law of Moses; on the other is a new Roman law (about the year 30 C.E., as the tradition tells it) that removed from the Sanhedrin the power of capital punishment. If Jesus takes compassion on the woman, he defies the law of Moses; if he follows the Jewish law, he defies the Roman government. He is stuck, or so they think. Until it becomes clear that the religious leaders, themselves, are on trial. A few select words by Jesus, and they silently steal away, knowing that their motives have been unveiled, knowing that there is nothing more they can do . . . for the moment. For the law of Moses is very clear about the integrity of witnesses: "You shall not spread a false report. You shall not join hands with the wicked to act as a malicious witness" (Ex 23:1). It is the scholar J.D.M. Derrett who hypothesizes that the woman's husband is in collusion with "the man caught in adultery," in order to destroy his wife.[7] Both of these, as well as the Pharisees themselves, are "malicious witnesses."

It remains to be noted that little is said about this woman's sin. That is not the real point of the story, except to reveal the compassion of Jesus. Rather, Jesus is challenging the Pharisees, and their sinful motives. In effect, he is holding up a mirror to everyone; compassion is there for the woman, to create a future where none existed before. And judgment is there for the religious leaders, guilty, by virtue of their leave-taking. In the end, it is only the woman who has remained; it is only the woman who is the recipient of divine compassion instead of the stones of human violence.

SOME RESOURCES
. . . .

Brown, Raymond E., SS, *The Gospel According to John.* Garden City, N.Y.: Doubleday, 1966.

O'Day, Gail R. "John," in *Women's Bible Commentary, Expanded Edition, With Apocrypha.* Edited by Carol A. Newsom and Sharon H. Ringe. Louisville, Ky.: Westminster John Knox Press, 1998, 381–93.

_____. The Word Disclosed. *John's Gospel and Narrative Preaching.* St. Louis: CBP Press, 1987.

Pearson, Helen Bruch. *Do What You Have the Power to Do: Studies of Six New Testament Women.* Nashville: Upper Room Books, 1992.

NOTES
. . . . .

1. 1 Peter 2:4.

2. 1 Peter 2:5.

3. See Deuteronomy 22:22; see also Leviticus 20:10.

4. This is from his diary, as quoted in National Catholic Reporter, March 9, 2001, p. 32.

5. Raymond E. Brown, SS, *The Gospel According to John* (Garden City, N.Y.: Doubleday, 1966), 335.

6. Brown, p. 336.

7. Brown, p. 338.

ten

ELIZABETH

We Bear the Spirit of the Living God

··

A Prayer Service on Elizabeth

···

This is a celebration of God's Spirit within each of us. Elizabeth is a prototype for us, for she is filled with the Spirit of God. As such, she is the first prophet in Luke's gospel, though Luke does not name her thus. To see and to honor the Spirit in us, the worship space ideally is set up with two semi-circles facing one another. At one end of the semi-circles, there is a large space that will provide a focus for the service. A large "spirit table" is within that space, with a scripture stand just to one side of the table. Musicians and a woman will occupy the chairs closest to the table at one side, and Elizabeth, the leader, and lector will occupy the chairs closest to the table on the other (near the scripture stand). There is a microphone on either side of the table for their use.

There are plants and red streamers throughout the worship space. The following items will also be used during the service: a large red table-cloth, two large candles, a plant, a bowl of water, a portable scripture stand, and the Book of Scripture.

Ministers: *"Elizabeth," a woman, leader of prayer, a lector, musicians, and cantor*

Materials: *Spirit table, scripture stand, two microphones, plants, red streamers, large red tablecloth, two large candles, bowl of water, scripture*

GATHERING RITES
. . . .

CALL TO WORSHIP *(Please stand.)*
. . . .

Leader: What will it take to melt the hearts of bleak midwinter?

All: Only the bounding, boundless Spirit of God,
blazing a way through the wilderness,
kindling repentance . . . a turning . . .
and seeing anew what love can do.

Leader: What will it take to ignite God's Spirit?

All: Only the boldness to be
enlarged and engorged with love,
pregnant, preparing to burst forth
upon this waiting, wintry world.

Leader: What will it take to set this world on fire?

All: Only the persistence to become
bearers of God's Holy Spirit
to the "little ones" who wait, trembling, with God, for justice.

Leader: O God-with-us, Spirit of God in human flesh,

All: Make of us your tender, bold ones,
breathing peace into fragile war-torn places,
blazing love into brittle, barren spaces,
blossoming like springtime along your holy way.
Amen.

"Until you have been clothed with power from on high."

OPENING HYMN

. . . .

or (during Advent)

During the opening hymn, there will be an entrance procession as follows. Two people carrying the tablecloth up high, in tent fashion, will lead the procession. They will be followed by the two candle-bearers, the two people carrying the scripture and the portable scripture stand, two people carrying a bowl of water and a plant, Elizabeth and "a woman," and the lector and leader of prayer. The procession will take time, so that each pair can place appropriate items on the table. Each of the pair carrying the tablecloth moves to either side of the table, lifts and billows the cloth, and places it on the table. They move to either side of the table and wait. The next pair places the candles on either side of the table and moves next to the first pair. The third pair places the stand and scripture on the table, moves to either side of the table, and waits. The fourth pair places the water and plant on the table and follows suit. The remaining four stand in front of the table and are joined by the waiting pairs. They bow and then take their places.

Liturgy of the Word

. . . .

Please be seated.

READING: Luke 1:5–25

. . . .

MUSICAL RESPONSE

. . . .

"Until you have been clothed with power from on high."

Elizabeth

171

Elizabeth: How will I ever find meaning in life without my heart's desire? A son! Oh, how I long for a son!

Woman: "Why is God punishing Elizabeth? Why has she been unable to bear a son?" There was the gossip, you know. The whispers behind Elizabeth's back. The questions of the villagers. Who would then often add, "Elizabeth seems like such a wise woman. You know, so right with God. She's even descended from Aaron and his priestly line. And her husband, Zechariah, is a priest, one of our most faithful, in fact. But she must have done something wrong. Why else would she be barren all these years?"

Elizabeth: It's been hard. I know about all the whispers. And the judgments. But I also know God's not punishing me. Why? Because of our stories. Take Hannah, for example. Now *there* was a woman who taught us all, the men included, how to pray. Persistently. Who taught us well about the upside-down, surprising ways of God. Who was filled, in the end, with the biggest surprise of all . . . a son! Samuel, a great man, the last of our judges. Then, of course, there's Elijah. My favorite prophet. So fiery and passionate! So faithful, even during Israel's darkest hour . . . the reign of King Ahab. He's the king, you remember, who "did evil in the sight of the Lord more than all who were before him."[1] Who chose to worship the puny gods of the Canaanites, the Baals, rather than the great God of Israel. How well I remember Elijah's challenge to these Baals, despite his fear! I remember, too, Elijah's compassion for the widow of Zarephath. Actually, they fed each other. Her meager supply of flour and oil never ran out; his praying, pleading breath restored her only son to life. It was all God's doing, of course.

Yes, these stories matter, for I live here in the hill country of Judea. The spine, the backbone of our homeland. It's here that the prophetic dream has been kept alive. It's here that we've managed to remember . . . at least in bits and pieces . . . what it means to be God's people. Faithful. Courageous. Passionate for justice. Compassionate to the widow, the orphan, and the stranger, for we were once strangers ourselves in a strange land. I know our stories. And I know that our God will never fail us.

Musical refrain:	*"O Breathe on Me, O Breath of God," verse 2.*
Woman:	Yes, Elizabeth never lost hope in the God who cared for her. We all knew something was up when Zechariah returned from his priestly duty. He who had never been at a loss for words was suddenly mute. It was his gesturing that told the story. They were to have a son! Their prayers had been heard! And Elizabeth became known for miles around as the righteous one.[2] Or simply Elizabeth, which means, "God is fullness."
Elizabeth:	It's true! God is my fullness! I needed time . . . and I took time, nearly five months . . . simply to be . . . to give thanks . . . to seek wisdom . . . to remember the stories once again . . . and, to vow to pass them on to my son.

Then, not long afterward, I heard a familiar voice at my doorstep. It was Mary! All the way from up north in Galilee. Nearly a hundred miles! At the sound of her voice I felt life! My son . . . and the Spirit of God . . . in a dance! Oh, I had long known the slow dance of lament. But this dance was pure joy. And before I knew what was happening, truth came tumbling out of my mouth. How "blessed is the fruit of your womb!"[3] A blessing on Mary. Instantly, an ancient memory flashed before me. Moses was blessing our people in the wilderness with those exact same words.[4] *If* they heard and acted on God's word. With Mary, no conditions were necessary. She was already full of God. Pregnant with the Word of God, the promised one, the Lord.[5] How this could be, I didn't know. But I believed.

"Until you have been clothed with power from on high."

More words tumbled out of the solitude of my soul. "Blessed is she who believed that there would be a fulfillment of what was spoken to her by the Lord."[6] A blessing on Mary's trust in the midst of such turmoil, for sure. But. Was it also a blessing on my barrenness, now become fullness? On all the impossibilities of God that Mary and I could not yet even begin to fathom? I had no idea. But I knew this. My cry had pierced the heavens. "How will I ever find meaning in life without my heart's desire?" And the heavens were only beginning to rain blessings on that question.

Musical refrain: *"O Breathe on Me, O Breath of God," verse 3.*

Woman: When it was her time, Elizabeth gave birth to a beautiful son. But, right from the beginning, this child created a disturbance. Or, I should say, it was Elizabeth who stirred things up. She named her son. That was unheard of! It was the father who did the naming. It had always been done that way. On top of that, she named him John . . . "Yahweh is graciousness" . . . and there was no John in their family. This has to be a mistake! But his father, still mute, gestured truth again . . . by writing on a tablet, "His name is John."[7] With that, Zechariah's mouth was opened, in praise of God. And ours were simply left open, in amazement and awe. "What then will this child become?"[8]

Elizabeth: John was a question, like every child who comes into this world. A question that takes a lifetime to answer. But this much I knew. We would treasure him. And feed him with the stories of our people. Yes, John would be full of my prophetic spirit . . . and the prickly passion of Elijah. He would develop a bond with Mary's son, a bond that had already begun. As for the rest, there was just no telling. Though there were signs, even now. An image had begun to take shape within me . . . of a highway through the wilderness.[9] What did it mean? I didn't know. Only time . . . and faithfulness to God's Spirit would tell.

. . . .

"If You Believe and I Believe," text is Zimbabwean traditional, tune is Zimbabwean traditional; adapt. of English traditional, as taught by Tarasai; arr. by John L. Bell, © 1991, Iona Community. GIA Publications, exclusive North American agent.

Ritual of the Laying on Hands
. . . .

Leader: Elizabeth. Barren woman who endured disgrace. Faithful woman, in right relationship with God, confident that God cared for her. Prophetic, spirited woman, announcer of God's Word. Her soul-searching question of meaning had to do with a son. Our search for meaning is no less significant, no less Spirit-filled. For some, it's a question of enduring and moving beyond the disgrace of poverty's clench . . . or the death-grip of addiction . . . or the rejection, by official church leaders, of precious women, called and gifted for ordination. For others, it's a question of strenuously grappling with structures in need of reform. Like Elizabeth, we all need the strengthening breath of God's Holy Spirit.

And like Elizabeth, we can trust that this Spirit is alive at our deepest core. That the life-changing, world-transforming breath of God . . . is ready to ignite our lives . . . and fan the flame of truth-seeking, courage, creativity, compassion, and justice-doing within and among us. Like Elizabeth and Mary, we can act in partnership with our God and one another to this end.

Take a quiet moment now and recall that the "Spirit intercedes with sighs too deep for words" on our behalf.[10] In that Spirit, invite God to help you name what you most need for the sake of our world. Then, following the prayer leaders, come up two by two and prayerfully inspirit one another by the laying on of hands. This may be done silently . . . or by naming to one another any specific, or general, need of God's Holy Spirit.

"Until you have been clothed with power from on high."

Elizabeth

MUSIC DURING THE RITUAL

"Veni, Sancte Spiritus," text is *Come Holy Spirit* with verses drawn from the Pentecost Sequence; Taize Community, 1978; tune by Jacques Berthier, © 1979, Les Presses de Taize, GIA Publications, Inc., agent.

and

"Spirit Blowing Through Creation," text and tune by Marty Haugen, © 1987, GIA Publications, Inc.

Closing Rites

Please stand.

BLESSING BY ALL

Leader invites each "half" of the assembly to turn and face the other, extending a hand in blessing, as all say the following:

Daughters and sons of God,
on whom the Spirit of God has hovered, breathed, and shown favor,
blessed are you, for you hear and do the word of God.
Spirit of God, ignite and enflame us, once again.
Mark us as your very own,
crackling with life,
that we might warm frozen hearts,
and subvert frozen structures
for the sake of your reign and your kindom.[11]
This we ask, in communion with you,
source of all life, Eternal Word, and Holy Spirit,
both now and forever. Amen.

CLOSING HYMN

"Canticle of the Turning," text by Rory Cooney, based on Luke 1:46–58; tune, STAR OF THE COUNTY DOWN, is Irish traditional, arr. by Rory Cooney, © 1990, GIA Publications, Inc.

"Until you have been clothed with power from on high."

Elizabeth

She has never quite emerged from the shadows. Rather, she has most often been glimpsed from afar, distant to us, peeking out from behind the stories of Zechariah, John the Baptist, and Mary, the mother of Jesus. She is secondary, mentioned almost without thought. Yet Elizabeth epitomizes her name, which means, "My God is fullness." In her very person she reveals many of the themes of Luke's gospel: righteousness, the return of God's Holy Spirit, joy, prophesy, witness to Jesus as the Christ, grace, the mercy and salvation of God, and prayer. She even fulfills a purpose of Luke in writing his gospel. For, in the poetic words of one commentator, "Luke wants his readers to imbibe hearty droughts of the joy, trust, faith, hope, endurance, expectation, and exultation of those who responded to the faithful God's actions in their lives."[12] Elizabeth has imbibed deeply, enough to be filled with God's Holy Spirit.

Yes, it is true that she appears in Luke's gospel overture, most often called the Infancy Narrative. And it is true that Luke's purpose here is to write a gospel in miniature, setting out the themes of his gospel in full. As such, it is Jesus, the Christ, who is the focus. And Luke's main purpose in writing is to deepen people's faith in this Jesus. Nonetheless, what has been generally overlooked is Elizabeth's role as prophet . . . and as one who prefigures Jesus in significant ways. It shall be the purpose of this short essay to bring her out of the shadows into her own.

Elizabeth is named, and that, in and of itself, is important.[13] Also, from the very beginning, she is described as "righteous," a pious Jew in right relationship with God, along with her husband Zechariah. Why is this so important? For Luke, righteousness points to Jesus, the crucified Christ. The centurion, taking in the meaning of Jesus' death on the cross, confesses faith in Jesus as the "righteous" or "innocent" one.[14] Immediately following this proclamation, Joseph of Arimathea is also described as "righteous."[15] For he has been "waiting expectantly for the kingdom of

God," and tenderly takes care of Jesus' body.[16] But, Elizabeth is the only woman in the entire New Testament who is named in this way.[17]

Luke never says this in so many words, but Elizabeth is also a prophet. For Luke assures us that she is "filled with the Holy Spirit" at the sound of Mary's greeting.[18] According to scripture scholar Joseph Fitzmyer, being filled with the Holy Spirit "denotes the gift of God's creative or prophetic presence."[19] And immediately she cries out, like Jesus in his dying words on the cross.[20] In the process, she utters several Spirit-filled truths. She blesses Mary, her young relative, soul-mate, and the God-bearer, then blesses the fruit of her womb. This second blessing, in effect, compares Mary to the people of Israel, who had been similarly blessed by Moses *if* "you will only obey the Lord your God, by diligently observing all his commandments that I am commanding you today."[21] Only, in Mary's case, no condition is necessary, for Elizabeth recognizes Mary as symbolic of the *faithful* people of God. Indeed, she blesses Mary for believing "that there would be a fulfillment of what was spoken to her by the Lord."[22] In this, she prefigures the words of Jesus himself, on the road to Jerusalem, when he returns a blessing from a woman in the crowd: "Blessed . . . are those who hear the word of God and obey it!"[23] Furthermore, Elizabeth is the first person and the only woman to make a christological profession of faith in this entire gospel. "And why has this happened to me, that the mother of my *Lord* comes to me?"[24] And finally, Elizabeth does something highly unusual for a woman of her day. She names her son, normally the prerogative of the father. And she names him John, even though there is no John in their family. Surely, the people think, there is a mistake! But, no, Zechariah, who at that point is still mute, writes on a tablet, "His name is John."[25] And all the people are amazed, a reaction that people often have to Jesus.

Elizabeth is most often recognized, of course, as an older barren woman, who is favored by God with her heart's desire, a son. And this son would become known as John the Baptist. She is also known as Mary's older relative and the wife of Zechariah, the priest. But, it must finally be said, that even in these more familiar roles, she proves herself an extraordinary woman of Spirit. For, we are also told that she, herself, has the blood of Aaron's priestly line flowing through her veins. And that she lives in the hill country of Judah, the place where the pre-monarchic ideals of covenant

"Until you have been clothed with power from on high."

relationship with God have taken strong root.[26] She is, therefore, a pious Jew who knows her tradition well. And she chooses to be influenced by and reflect the best of her tradition in her role as mother. Let me explain.

Elizabeth has often been associated with barren women from the Hebrew scripture, whom God has ultimately gifted with their heart's desire, a son. Sarah, conceiving at eighty-nine years of age, is the ultimate example that nothing is "too wonderful for the Lord."[27] Others include Rachel and Hannah. But Sarah, Rachel, and Hannah are caught in a systemic web of rivalry with another "wife," and are haunted by anguish, jealousy, and competition.[28] According to scripture scholar Athalya Brenner, their stories instruct us in one way of understanding the "birth of a hero" narrative.[29]

But, there was another way, a way of conspiracy for life. A way of cooperation and generosity, of unconditional love and courage, despite differences in culture and religious background. This was the way, for example, of the three women surrounding the birth of Moses: Jochebed, his birth mother; the daughter of Pharaoh, his adoptive mother; and Miriam, his sister, perhaps twelve at the time.[30] Jochebed took an enormous risk rooted in unconditional love to send this precious three-month-old child of her womb down the river in a tiny ark, as the only hope of saving his life. And Pharaoh's compassionate daughter risked the wrath of her father, who had ordered the murder of all Hebrew baby boys, by pulling this treasured child out of the water to freedom and life. But it took the young Miriam, who courageously watched and waited during the night, to connect the two mothers. Women who might otherwise have been enemies became conspirators for life . . . and ultimately the freedom of a people. In a similar way, Ruth breathed life back into the withered, bitter, barren Naomi. The widowed daughter-in-law Ruth, an Edomite, followed her widowed mother-in-law Naomi back to Bethlehem, adopting Naomi's people and God as her very own. Indeed, she even embodied her new-found covenant God, "Where you go, I will go; where you lodge, I will lodge. . . ."[31]

Surely, in some way, Elizabeth was deeply formed, like this latter group, by the grace and Spirit of God. She never gave into the temptation to rage against her neighbors who found her wanting in her barrenness . . . or against her God. And she only had praise and support for her younger relative, whom she named—prophetically—the mother of her Lord. She understood power as Jesus would draw upon and release it . . . the power of God's Spirit for healing, courage, and life.

In sum, Elizabeth is a woman who bears God's Spirit. A woman of prayer. A woman of justice, or right relationship with God and people. A woman of hope, courage, and joy. A prophet. A model of discipleship for women and men of any age.

SOME RESOURCES

Fitzmyer, Joseph A., SJ. *The Gospel According to Luke, I-IX.* Garden City, N.Y.: Doubleday, 1981.

Karris, Robert J., OFM. "The Gospel According to Luke," in *The New Jerome Biblical Commentary* edited by Raymond E. Brown, SS, Joseph A. Fitzmyer, SJ, Roland E. Murphy, O Carm. Englewood Cliffs, N. J.: Prentice Hall, 1990, 675–721.

Reid, Barbara E. *Choosing the Better Part?: Women in the Gospel of Luke.* Collegeville, Minn.: Liturgical Press, A Michael Glazier Book, 1996.

Schaberg, Jane. "Luke," in *Women's Bible Commentary, Expanded Edition, With Apocrypha* edited by Carol A. Newsom and Sharon H. Ringe. Louisville, Ky.: Westminster John Knox Press, 1998, 363–80.

NOTES

1. See 1 Kings 16:30.

2. See Luke 1:6. According to Barbara Reid, Elizabeth was the only woman so named in the entire New Testament. This was a title that the writer of Luke/Acts used of Jesus three times in the Acts of the Apostles (3:14, 7:52, 22:14). See Barbara E. Reid, *Choosing the Better Part?: Women in the Gospel of Luke* (Collegeville, Minn.: Liturgical Press, A Michael Glazier Book, 1996), 58–59.

3. See Luke 1:42.

4. See Deuteronomy 28:4.

5. See Luke 1:43. Elizabeth is the first prophet of Luke's gospel; she is the first in Luke's gospel to name Jesus as *Kyrios*, the Greek word for Lord. Barbara Reid notes on p. 72 that this title is one of Luke's favorites for Jesus; he uses it ninety-seven times.

"Until you have been clothed with power from on high."

6. Luke 1:45.

7. See Luke 1:63.

8. See Luke 1:66.

9. See Isaiah 40:3.

10. See Romans 8:26.

11. This term for the "kingdom" of God was coined by Latin American women theologians. It denotes relationship.

12. Robert J. Karris, OFM, "The Gospel According to Luke," in *New Jerome Biblical Commentary*, edited by Raymond, E. Brown, SS, Joseph A. Fitzmyer, SJ, and Roland E. Murphy, O Carm. (Englewood Cliffs, N.J.: Prentice Hall, 1990), 679.

13. According to Jane Schaberg, only ten women are named in the Gospel of Luke, compared to thirty-nine men named in the story and another ninety-four men named in the genealogy of Jesus. See Jane Schaberg, "Luke," in *Women's Bible Commentary*, *Expanded Edition*, *With Apocrypha*, edited by Carol A. Newsom and Sharon H. Ringe (Louisville, Ky.: Westminster John Knox Press, 1998), 368.

14. See Luke 1:6 and 23:47. In both instances the Greek word *dikaios*, meaning *righteous*, is used.

15. Luke 23:50.

16. Luke 23:51.

17. Reid, pp. 58–59.

18. Luke 1:41.

19. Joseph A. Fitzmyer, SJ, *The Gospel According to Luke I-IX*, (Garden City, N.Y.: Doubleday, 1981), 326.

20. See Luke 1:42 and Luke 23:46.

21. See Deuteronomy 28:1, 4.

22. See Luke 1:45.

23. See Luke 11:28.

24. Luke 1:43, my emphasis. The Greek for Lord is *Kyrios*, a favorite christological term of Luke's.

25. Luke 1:63.

26. Scripture scholar Bernhard Anderson notes that the Confederacy of the Judges (ca. 1200–1020 B.C.E.) was bound together by common devotion of the twelve tribes to Yahweh, God of the Covenant. See Bernard W. Anderson, *Understanding the Old Testament*, *Third Edition* (Englewood Cliffs, N.J.: Prentice Hall, 1975), 155.

27. Genesis 18:14.

28. See Genesis, chapters 16 and 21:1–21; Genesis 29:1–30:24, 35:16–20; and 1 Samuel 1:1–2:10 and 21.

29. See Reid, pp. 73–74. She relies upon the work of Athalya Brenner, "Female Social Behavior: Two Descriptive Patterns Within the 'Birth of the Hero' Paradigm," VT 36 (1986): 257–73.

30. See Exodus 2:1–10.

31. Ruth 1:16.

"Until you have been clothed with power from on high."

eleven

BRIGIT OF IRELAND

We Are Formed in the Image of Christ

. . . .

A Service on Brigit of Ireland[1]

. . . .

INTRODUCTION
. . . .

This prayer service might be celebrated on or near February 1, St. Brigit's feast day. To her ancient ancestors, this day was known as Imbolc, the first sign of spring after the "dead month" of January. For us Christians, this time of year stands at the head of the Lenten season. Lent means springtime, a season of Christian preparation for new life in all its fullness. It is a final formation time for catechumens and candidates[2] who are preparing for full initiation into the church, as well as a time of renewal and reconciliation for all who form the Body of Christ.

With this in mind, it is worth noting that the Celtic storytellers of old . . . those who spun the tales of the fifth to seventh century Irish saints . . . conformed those lives to the pattern of Christ. From early on, Christians had proclaimed that the Spirit of Christ lives on fully in male and female . . . that woman as well as man fully reveals the pattern of

Christ.[3] In other words, woman, as well as man, is capable of revealing the divine. For Celtic Christians, that belief had been deeply imbedded in the tales of their ancient goddesses, and of the triple goddess Brigit, in particular.[4] Indeed, the fifth century St. Brigit became a seamless garment of ancient divinity, clothed now in Christ. This prayer service, then, provides a welcome way to celebrate both female and male formation in Christ's image.

Ideally, this service would be celebrated during ordinary time before Lent begins, so that the focus of the environment is the baptismal font (or other large, clear vessel of water). Around this is a large white Christ "cloak" or shawl, artfully draped in some fashion, the Christ candle, and the oils of the church. There might also be a plant or some kind of greenery, further symbolizing life.

Ministers: a leader, two "Irish" storytellers, lector(s), musicians, and cantor

Materials: baptismal font, large white Christ "cloak," Christ candle, oils of the church, some kind of greenery

Gathering Rites

• •

CALL TO WORSHIP[5]
• • • • • • • • • • • • • • • •

Leader:	Come, The Three Who are over us,
All:	O Come, The Three Who are below us,
Leader:	Come, The Three Who are above us here,
All:	O Come, The Three Who are above us yonder;
Leader:	Come, The Three Who are in the earth,
All:	O Come, The Three Who are in the air,
Leader:	Come, The Three Who are in the heaven,
All:	O Come, The Three Who are in the great pouring sea,

Leader: We are placing our soul and our body under your guiding this day,

All: Protector of earth and of heaven, of sea and of sky, of all that is known and unknown, both now and forever. Amen.

OPENING HYMN

"God Has Chosen Me," text and tune by Bernadette Farrell, © 1990, Bernadette Farrell. Published by OCP Publications.

Liturgy of the Word

FIRST READING: WISDOM 7:24–26

PSALM 16

"You Will Show Me the Path of Life," Refrain 1, text by Marty Haugen, based on Psalm 16:1–2, 6–10; tune by Marty Haugen, © 1988, GIA Publications, Inc.

SECOND READING: GALATIANS 3:26–28

ALLELUIA

"Celtic Alleluia," text by Christopher Walker, tune by Fintan O'Carroll and Christopher Walker, © 1985, Fintan O'Carroll and Christopher Walker. Published by OCP Publications.

GOSPEL: JOHN 14:12–14

REFLECTION (Two Storytellers)

Voice 1:   Once there was a woman bright as the sun. A fiery arrow, according to legend, direct in making her mark. A healer . . . kind and compassionate. Yet strong, powerful, and creative. Capable of governing large numbers of people. Respected by the male hierarchy of the church in her day. So, of course, word of her spread everywhere, and could not be contained.

Voice 2:   Who was this extraordinary woman? Why, none other than St. Brigit of Ireland. St. Brigit of the fifth century. St. Brigit, whose name means "exalted." Brilliant enough, holy enough to form a sacred trinity with the likes of St. Patrick and St. Columcille.

Voice 1:   It seems that her public ministry began like this. She was so inspired by the new monasteries of her day that she longed to form one of her own. Why? Because they were centers of church and belonging, of crafts and farming. They were places of rest and reflection for some. Or, places to work in satisfaction for sins . . . and even crime, for others. So, off she went, to a very rich man with her request. His response? You may have as much land as your cloak will cover. And the miracle was that her cloak expanded and expanded, as it touched ground, claiming a wide sweeping territory for Christ. That land became famous as Cill-Dara, or Kildare, the Cell of the Oak. A double monastery of men and women, a place of charity, artistry, and economic self-sufficiency.[6]

Voice 2:   But let's go back to the beginning. In her case, back to the ancient goddess Brigit. For where the saint begins and the goddess ends is not at all clear. In the Ireland of old, you see, it was woman . . . in the form of goddesses . . . who opened the window onto God's mothering care for all. And Brigit outshone them all. She was Virgin Mother, Lawgiver,[7] "the 'good female' principle personified."[8] The only force capable of uniting the various tribes. She was patroness of poets, spinners, and weavers. A woman of hospitality and compassion. Rooted in the land and in the hearts of her people.

Voice 1:   But in the fifth century this goddess encountered the Christ. And the Gospel according to St. Brigit was born. It began, just like two gospels of Jesus, with an infancy narrative. As the story goes, Brigit's father, a pagan chieftain named Dubthach, bought and impregnated a slave named Broiscech.[9] But the wife of Dubthach threatened to leave him, with her dowry, if he did not sell this slave. Immediately! To someone far away! Dubthach sadly agreed. But as he and Broicsech were making their way to a far off place, a druid suddenly appeared out of nowhere. Pointing to Broicsech, he solemnly pronounced, "Marvelous will be the child that is in her womb. No one on earth will be like her."[10] Indeed, "the offspring of your wife shall serve the offspring of the slave, for this slave will bring forth a wonderful radiant daughter who will shine like the sun among the stars of heaven."[11] And it was so. For, it is said that immediately upon Brigit's birth, she was brought to the queen, whose son had just died. When Brigit was placed on top of the dead boy, her breath restored him to life.[12]

MUSICAL REFRAIN

● ● ● ● ● ● ● ● ● ● ● ● ●

"Behold, I Make All Things New," text and tune from the Iona Community, © 1995, Iona Community. GIA Publications, Inc., exclusive North American agent.

Voice 2:   Yes, signs and wonders followed her everywhere, from the time she was an infant. For it is said that Broicsech went off to milk the cows soon after her daughter's birth, leaving Brigit sleeping soundly in her little bed. Immediately the neighbors "saw the house on fire, as if a single flame reached from earth to heaven. When they came to rescue her, the fire disappeared, but they saw it as a sign" of the Holy Spirit in Brigit.[13] And the Spirit was with her, indeed! For a wizard had a dream about her baptism. There were three angels, anointing her head with oil and completing the sacrament of baptism over her. It was the third angel who named her Sancta Brigita, that is, Saint Brigit.

Voice 1:   And her ministry was so much like that of Jesus. She was a healer, always in touch with the needs of others. Even a wounded healer. One day, as the story goes,

"Until you have been clothed with power from on high."

Brigit of Ireland   189

Brigit fell out of a chariot and "hit her head against a stone. She was severely wounded and the blood gushed out. Two women who were lying on the road were healed by that blood."[14] On another occasion, she ministered to "four sick persons in the church: a consumptive man, a lunatic, a blind man, and a leper;" and "they were healed from their diseases."[15]

Is it any surprise that this happened on Holy Thursday night?

Voice 2:   Then, of course, there are all the favorite stories. Here's mine. It is said that the day came for Brigit to receive the veil of religious life. She held back out of humility, to be last among her sisters. At that very moment, a "fiery pillar rose from her head to the (rooftop) of the church. Then Bishop Mel called to her, 'Come, O holy Brigit, that a veil may be [placed on your head] before the other virgins.' It came to pass then, through the grace of the Holy Ghost, that the form of ordaining a Bishop was read out over Brigit."[16] When Mac-caille, Bishop Mel's assistant, protested that this was impossible for a woman, the bishop proclaimed that he had nothing to do with it. For the Spirit of God had spoken the final word. And so it was that Brigit's successors, the abbesses of Kildare, would be presented with her shepherd's staff upon their installation.

Voice 1:   And *I* enjoy these tales of Brigit. There was the time when Brigit went to a well, drew out water, and blessed it, "so that it turned into the taste of ale, and she gave it to her nurse, who straightway became whole."[17] And then there was the time when St. Patrick came to her monastery to preach. A huge crowd gathered 'round, to hear him. Someone pointed out to Brigit that there wasn't nearly enough to feed such a huge crowd, only "one sheep, and twelve loaves, and a little milk."[18] So Brigit blessed and broke what was there . . . passed it around . . . and gathered up more than they had started with.

Voice 2:   There she is. St. Brigit. A woman bright as the sun. Bright as the Son, Jesus. A woman who knew that the

WALKING WITH WISDOM'S DAUGHTERS

"Until you have been clothed with power from on high."

reign of God is at hand. In all the thin places of earth, sea, and sky. And ultimately, in the coming of her very own resurrection day. For, when her days were over, "after founding and helping cells and churches and altars in abundance, after miracles and marvels whose number is as the sand of sea, or stars of heaven, after charity and mercy"[19] in abundance, she celebrated her approaching resurrection with communion from Nindid Pure-hand of Rome. It is said that "her soul is like a sun in the heavenly Kingdom."[20] And that she shall rise at the end, in union with the Blessed Trinity, "like a shining lamp in completeness of body and soul."[21]

Musical Refrain: "Behold, I Make All Things New," as before.

Ritual of Empowerment into Christ
· ·

Leader: Formation in Christ does not just happen once, on our day of baptism. It happens daily, as we forever meet the challenge of what it means to put on Christ. And it happens to women, as fully as it does to men. If you are willing to commit to this ongoing formation in Christ, please respond affirmatively to the following, and then come to the water of new birth, once again, to be wrapped in the "cloak" of Christ.

Leader: Do you believe that in Christ, "there is no longer Jew or Greek, there is no longer slave or free, there is no longer male and female, for all of you are one in Christ Jesus?"[22]

All: I do believe.

Leader: Do you believe that woman, as well as man, is fully clothed in Christ?

All: I do believe.

Leader: Do you believe that, just as St. Brigit spread her cloak over the land in order to claim her territory for Christ, we are to spread our Christ cloaks over our corners of the world for the sake of God's reign?

All:	I do believe.
Leader:	Are you willing to commit yourself to this active clothing in Christ, for the sake of God's reign, here and now?
All:	I am.
Leader:	To seal this commitment, then, please come forward. As the cloak of Christ is wrapped around you, pray silently or aloud for whatever you need to strengthen this commitment. Then affirm your promise by saying "Amen."

MUSIC DURING THE RITUAL

"Song Over the Waters," text and tune by Marty Haugen, © 1987, GIA Publications, Inc.

and/or

"Ruah," text and tune by Liam Lawton, from the collection *In the Quiet,* © 2002, GIA Publications, Inc.

Sending Forth Rites

BLESSING

Leader:	Bless to us our eyes this day,
All:	to glimpse the shimmerings and glimmerings of God in every tear, smile, leaf, creature, and universe.
Leader:	Bless to us our ears this day,
All:	to attend the symphony of the divine in perfect harmony and attend to the groans of unfinished creation.
Leader:	Bless to us our wills this day,
All:	to invigorate our desire for transformation in conformity with the divine.

Leader: Bless to us our hearts this day,

All: to ignite a holy blaze for justice
           and a warming glow of compassion.

Leader: Bless to us our hands this day,

All: to do the work of God in our world
           according to our gifted passions.

Leader: Bless to us our humanity this day,

All: to more fully become the eyes,
           ears, wills, hearts, and hands of Christ.

           Amen!

CLOSING HYMN

• • • • • • • • • • • • •

"*Song of St. Patrick*," text by Marty Haugen, based on *St. Patrick's Breastplate*, tune by Marty Haugen, © 1986, GIA Publications, Inc.[23]

Brigit of Ireland

• •

St. Brigit is a mystery. Where she begins and the ancient goddess Brigit ends is not clear. Indeed, "many scholars have exhausted their energies trying to distinguish between Brigit as goddess, saint, or folklore figure, only to realize that the distinction is a fruitless one to begin with."[24] In part, this may result from the fact that the goddess legends were not committed to writing until the time of the fifth-century saint. The result was a seamless garment of goddess and woman formed in the image of Christ, "an extraordinarily powerful, loving, and vital person. She is a bundle of contradictions that add up to a singular whole, a personage of fire and water, of will and compassion, intensely focused on her mission of protection and care for her people. She is a healer who is also a warrior, a humble milk-maid who commands miracles from God, a goddess of fertility best known to Catholics as a holy virgin."[25]

This much is clear. Her storytellers intentionally shaped her life . . . like that of other Celtic saints . . . around that of Jesus . . . a "Gospel according to Brigid," as it were. St. Brigit of Ireland is the product of Christian hagiography, an art form or literary genre "written to present the saints as worthy spiritual mentors who can inspire us" to live as they have lived.[26] It is not factual history, as we understand it today. Rather, it is myth, in the best sense of the word, like much of scripture. That is, it contains profound levels of truth, particularly with regard to God, humanity, and human relationship with God, and all of creation. This brief exploration will include a look at the ancient goddess traditions, a synopsis of St. Brigit's life, the Christ-like legends that developed around her, and her unique reflection of Celtic spirituality.

BRIGIT, THE GODDESS

The earliest Irish ancestors worshipped gods and goddesses, connected to the entire kaleidoscope of life . . . ocean and sky, river and landscape, animal, plant, and human. Goddesses were essential, for they captured the essence of life . . . bleeding that did not end in death . . . birthing and the creative arts . . . and rivers that appeared to be womb openings to life beyond.[27] Some of the goddesses had a triple form . . . the spiral of birth, life, and death . . . still captured in the art of the Irish people. Only a triple goddess, it was thought, could do justice to the complexity of the divine and the wonder of life itself. And Brigit, the triple goddess whose name means "high" or "exalted,"[28] would eventually tower over them all. In fact, variations on her name are found throughout Europe. Brigantia, for example, is the Latin form of Brigit. Who was this ancient goddess? Where did she come from? And how did she hold sway over so many others?

When the warring, patriarchal Celtic tribes poured into Ireland from their homeland of Galatia, they found "a matrifocal land where the relationship of the mother formed one of the central principles of social organization."[29] Goddesses mattered, as deities capable of nurturing and sustaining life. According to Mary

Condren, the Celtic tribes, with their feuding male tribal gods, needed a strong goddess to unite them in the centuries before Christianity. Brigit ultimately became the one . . . as triple goddess, Supreme Lawmaker of the Brehon Laws (the Irish counterpart of the Torah), and Mother goddess.[30]

Why Brigit? Legends abound, but the point of them all is this. Brigit alone was capable of crossing the chasms of various cultures and the warring Celtic tribes. "The name Brigit provided a language whereby warring tribes could communicate with each other through symbols and common allegiances to her memory."[31] Ancient legend has it that Brigit was one of the Tuatha de Danaan, or people of the goddess Danu.[32] Her mother may have been the goddess Boann (after whom the River Boyne was named). According to some tales (here named Brigh), she loved Bres the Beautiful, ruler of the Children of Danu. Because he was sometimes described as half Fomorian, the race ruling Ireland before the coming of the people of the goddess Danu, Brigit was proclaimed the mediator of the two races.[33] She also became mother goddess . . . the one who cared deeply about her people. In time, Brigit would take on the positive aspects of the ancient Irish goddesses Tephi, Danu, Macha, and the Morrigan, all of whom had been bound to the land.[34] To the Celts, then, Brigit was strong enough to bridge many a divide.

She seems, also, to have woven a creative, composite tapestry from the threads of several other goddesses . . . including Belisama, Juno (revered as Queen of Heaven, midwife, and goddess of love), Minerva (patron of Wisdom and handicraft), Isis, Vesta (goddess of the Vestal Virgins), and Sul. Three of Brigit's symbols, the vulture, serpent, and cow, were associated with the goddess Isis.[35] She had traits in common with Hecate, the ancient Greek goddess of liminality (capable, therefore, of crossing boundaries into another world). Ultimately, Brigit is a deity who spans all things: "fertility and birth; poetry and inspiration; the fires of the hearth, the forge, and the sun itself; the waters of springs, wells, and the very seas; the arts of rulership and the skills of war. She is Midwife and Lifegiver, Poet, Smith, Healer, Warrior and Sovereign."[36]

Brigit the Saint inherits her images and titles. Images of milk, fire (with flames bursting forth from her head, as they did from the goddess),[37] sun (whose rays surround the cross of Brigit), and serpents (symbolic of regeneration) make their way into the legends of the saint. As the story goes, for example, Saint Brigit is bathed in milk immediately after her birth, very likely as a sign of the divinity within her. And her Feast Day of Imbolc (February 1, the same day as that of the Roman goddess Juno) carries with it references to milking and images of breastfeeding. Imbolc, in fact, has been translated variously as "ewe-milk," "lustration," or "purification."[38] In addition, like the goddess, St. Brigit is recognized as patroness of poets. And it is said that the embroidery tools of St. Brigit (the symbols of the goddess Minerva) are preserved in a chapel near Glastonbury, England, for she is known as patroness of spinning and weaving. She is also known, like the goddess, for her generosity, hospitality, compassion, and healing. She is virgin, unbroken vessel, independent of any man, opposed to war and symbolic of the entire culture, like the vestal virgins of old. At the same time, she is still mother. For, to this day, there is a carving of "a sheela-no-gig (a figure holding the entrance to her womb wide open)" on the top of arch at the entrance to the medieval church at Killinaboy.[39] In effect, St. Brigit is inviting all to enter the church through her womb.

SAINT BRIGIT, THE WOMAN OF HISTORY

She is revered by the Irish as one of "the holy trinity of Irish saints," along with Patrick and Columcille. But it is not easy to piece together her life. For, in truth, Brigit has moved through the centuries, from goddess to saint to woman of legend. But this much we know. She was the daughter of Dubthach, a pagan chieftain, and his slave, a woman named Broicsech. Born in 452 C.E. (or thereabouts), her light radiates over Ireland until 524 C.E. (or thereabouts). This is the beginning of a golden age, the blossoming of Celtic spirituality and the rise of monasticism. Called the Age of the Saints, from the late fifth to the late seventh centuries, it is, simply, a time of beauty. Scholar Nora Chadwick says this: it expresses "the Christian ideal with a sanctity and a sweetness which have never been surpassed."[40] And Brigit outshines all other female church leaders of her day.

Founder and abbess of a double monastery at Kildare,[41] she presides over a community of nuns and a separate group of male clerics. In those days, monasteries are living organisms, providing the

"Until you have been clothed with power from on high."

basis of religious, economic, and social life in Ireland.[42] They become centers of learning . . . rooted in the psalms, other scripture, the classics, history, and letters. Some, like the monastic school of Lismore, draw many to their lamps of learning. They also provide hospitality and sanctuary for those in need . . . and allow penitents a means to make satisfaction for their sins *or* their crimes. They offer some the possibility of pursuing a religious . . . even ascetic . . . life. At the same time, whole families live and work within their grounds, supporting everyone by their labor. Cogitosus, one of Brigit's earliest hagiographers, describes a visit to her monastery in this way. "Who can list the chaotic crowds and countless folk who flock in from all the provinces: some for the abundance of food, others who are feeble seeking health, others just to look at the mobs, and still others who come with great gifts to the festival of Saint Brigid."[43]

And that great festival, or feast day, is still February 1, the Feast of Imbolc. It is one of four yearly feasts dating back to pagan times . . . Samhain (November 1, the beginning of winter, a time between chaos and order, between the "other world" and this world), Bealtaine (May 1, the beginning of summer), and Lughnasa (August 1, the beginning of autumn). As Imbolc becomes Christianized, it is revered as a threshold time, a crossing over into spring and new creation, after the "dead month" of January. And it also is said that Brigit makes way for the Feast of the Presentation of the Lord on February 2. Indeed, in legend, Brigit becomes known as foster-mother of both Jesus and his mother, Mary.

Quite a woman, this Brigit. Well known for her generosity of spirit, her hospitality and compassion, from which her healing power flows. At ease in living among, and hosting, the Church hierarchy. Even renowned as a bishop, herself.[44] She is, as well, that most important person in Celtic spirituality, a soul friend or *anamchara*. For the Irish know that "inner healing happens when we openly and honestly acknowledge to another person our concerns, grief, and spiritual diseases, and that God is very close to those who speak as friends do, heart to heart."[45]

"Until you have been clothed with power from on high."

FORMED IN THE IMAGE OF CHRIST

. . . .

It is no accident that Brigit's life, as we know it, is formed in the image of Christ. Even before she was born, there were signs and wonders . . . and announcements of the magnificent child about to enter this world, not unlike the divine announcement to Mary in Luke's gospel and to Joseph in Matthew.[46] And as with Jesus, a genealogy completes the infancy narrative of the "Gospel according to Brigid:"[47] Brigit is "daughter of Dubthach, son of Demre, son of Bresal, of the sept of Echaid Find Fuathnairt."[48]

From early on, as with Jesus, the Spirit of God radiated through Brigit.[49] The story is told that Brigit "was taken straightway after her birth to the queen's dead son, and when the girl's breath came to the son, he arose out of death."[50] And just as Jesus was claimed by a divine voice at his baptism, so too was Brigit claimed at her baptism.

She was holy; of that there is no doubt. "For on the day that Brigit was to receive the nun's veil, Bishop Mel was so moved by the Holy Spirit that he pronounced the words of ordination over her. Said Bishop Mel: 'No power have I in this matter. That dignity hath been given by God unto Brigid, beyond every (other) woman.' Wherefore the men of Ireland from that time to this give episcopal honour to Brigid's successor."[51]

As the story comes to us, Brigit was a wounded healer, just like Jesus. And like Jesus on the eve of his Passion, Brigit refused to use violence in any way. In fact, she enraged her father because she gave away his sword to a leper. (It is said that she was forever giving *something* away to those who were poor.) But *this* time her father was determined to sell Brigit to the king. It was Brigit's proclaimed desire to give everything to "the Lord of the elements" that saved her, for the king recognized her merit before God.[52]

Her miracle stories abound! And like those of Jesus, hers are rooted in compassion. On one occasion, not unlike the wedding feast of Cana, "Brigid went to a certain well, and filled her vessel thereat, and blessed (the water), so that it turned into the taste of ale, and she gave it to her nurse, who straightway became whole."[53] Furthermore, "everything to which her hand was set used to increase."[54] For example, when a guest came to Dubthach's house,

"Until you have been clothed with power from on high."

Brigit was given five pieces of bacon to be boiled. But, she took pity on a starving dog that made its way into the house. She gave the dog one, then another, piece of bacon. And when her father questioned her about the bacon, she told him to count the pieces. None were missing![55] And yet, these are only a few of the many "miracles and marvels" that "the Lord wrought for Brigid. So many are they that no one could declare them, unless her own soul or an angel of God should come to declare them."[56]

Furthermore, just like Jesus of John's gospel, Brigit remains an unbroken vessel. According to John's Passion account, the Jewish authorities "asked Pilate to have the legs of the crucified men broken and the bodies removed" because the Sabbath was approaching.[57] But the soldiers did not break Jesus' legs, for they saw that he was already dead.[58] Similarly, Brigit became known as the Unbroken Vessel, symbolizing the unity of Irish culture, despite the petty wars of kings and tribes. In fact, the Irish word for virgin, og, means "whole, untouched, intact, inviolate."[59] Because she belonged to nobody, she could, in effect, mediate for all. Finally, like Jesus and so many Irish saints, she has an intuition about the end of her earthly days.[60] And it is said, she will rise at the end, and live forever in union with the Blessed Trinity.

ROOTED IN THE FLAVOR OF CELTIC SPIRITUALITY

Celtic Christian spirituality flowered from the fifth to the twelfth centuries. It "was very much the child of the pagan culture which preceded it, one that valued poetic imagination and artistic creativity, kinship relations and the warmth of a hearth, the wonder of stories and the guidance of dreams."[61] It was a spirituality rooted in landscape, sea, and sky. A spirituality of hospitality to people and places. Brigit's delightful, practical prayer, according to legend, reflects this hospitality.

> I would wish a great lake of ale for the King of Kings; I would wish the family of Heaven to be drinking it through life and time. I would wish the men [sic] of Heaven in my own house; I would wish vessels of peace to be given to them. I would wish vessels full of alms to be given away; I would wish joy to be in their drinking; I would wish Jesus to be here among them. I

"Until you have been clothed with power from on high."

would wish the three Marys of great name; I would wish the people of Heaven from every side. I would wish to be a rent-payer to the Prince; that way if I was in trouble he would give me a good blessing.[62]

And according to legend, she was, indeed, granted all her wishes, for they were always conformed to the will of God.

Brigit is a woman of her day in that she finds God . . . indeed, looks for God . . . in all things, all creation, even in a tender relationship with animals. As the story goes, one day a foolish man killed the pet fox of the king. And the king, enraged over this senseless act, promised to kill the man in return unless another fox was found, as clever as his own. As soon as Brigit heard of this, she implored God to save the condemned man. Immediately God answered her prayer, sending her a wild fox. The fox landed in her lap, "nestling up under the fold of Brigid's garment."[63] Upon arrival at the court, Brigit pleaded for the release of the condemned man in exchange for this fox. It was done. The man was set free, and, not long after, the fox escaped, making his way home to his own cave. Because of this intimacy with all creation, Brigit and others prayed their way through the ordinary events of the day. Indeed, Brigit might well have inspired the following prayer, used during the milking of the cows. (It should be noted that Bride is another name for Brigit.) "Come, Mary, and milk my cow, Come Bride, and encompass her, Come, Columba the benign, and twine thine arms around my cow. . . . Come, Mary Virgin, to my cow, Come, great Bride, the beauteous, Come thou milkmaid of Jesus Christ, and place thine arms beneath my cow."[64] God is *always* to be found in the ordinary.

Women assumed a significant role in the Celtic Christian church. Unlike the Roman Church, which increasingly put limits on women's participation, the Celtic bishops "did not reject the fellowship and ministration of women."[65] Indeed, Brigit was probably regarded as an equal by male leaders of her day. A calendar dating from the year 800 names scores of monastic women worthy of remembrance.[66] Oh, it was true that society placed limits on a woman's inheritance. Any land she owned would pass to her kin at her death. She could only "hand on outside her kin that land which she received as a gift or gained for services rendered."[67] But, these limitations were nothing compared to Roman attitudes of the day. A sixth-century letter from bishops in Gaul to Irish missionaries makes the point, condemning the Irish practice of inviting women to participate in the distribution of the eucharist. "We appeal to your charity, not only to restrain *these little women* from staining the holy sacraments by administering them illicitly, but also not to admit to live under your roof any woman who is not your grandmother, your mother, your sister, or your niece."[68] Brigit did not escape these tensions, for legends abound of her efforts to seek Roman approval of her ordo, the book of ritual used at Kildare. But, through no fault of her own, Brigit's messenger was always stymied in delivering the message. Ultimately, however, by the twelfth century, the Roman order would prevail.

And yet, the spirit of Brigit/Brigid lives on and is not forgotten. It is a gentle yet assertive spirit. A spirit of creativity *and* administration. A spirit of soul friendship, storytelling, poetry, and artistry. A spirit of quiet contemplation, compassion, healing, and hospitality. A spirit of passionate action on behalf of those in need. A spirit of justice, that roams the land in lioness fashion, an advocate for human dignity, including the full stature of women in the church. It is the spirit that recognizes the "thin places," alert to the presence of God in the here and now. A spirit of soaring gratitude and joy, mingled with groaning lament over injustice and the suffering of the innocent. It is a spirit that listens for the symphony of the divine in the everyday and longs for the fullness of the divine in every adventure. It is a spirit imbedded in the Irish heart and soul.

SOME RESOURCES
. . . .

Anecdota Oxoniensia, "Life of Brigit," in *Lives of Saints from the Book of Lismore*, translated by Whitley Stokes, D.C.L. Oxford: Clarendon Press, 1890; facsimile reprint by Llanerch Publisher, Felinfach, 1995.

Azrael, Amber K. and Arynn K., *Candlemas: Feast of Flames, Brigit's Festival of Light and Life*. St. Paul, Minn.: Llewellyn Publications, 2001.

Chadwick, Nora K. *The Age of the Saints in the Early Celtic Church*. London: Oxford University Press, 1961.

Condren, Mary. *The Serpent and the Goddess: Women, Religion, and Power in Celtic Ireland*. San Francisco: Harper & Row, 1989.

De Waal, Esther, ed. *The Celtic Vision: Prayers and Blessings from the Outer Hebrides. Selections from the Carmina Gadelica*. Petersham, Mass.: St. Bede's Publications, 1990.

"*Until you have been clothed with power from on high.*"

Brigit of Ireland

Golden, Jonathan, "*An Turas*[69]: A Journey Into Celtic Spirituality." In *Spiritual Life*, Summer 1996, 136–49.

Hughes, Kathleen and Ann Hamlin. *Celtic Monasticism*. New York: The Seabury Press, 1981.

Lawton, Liam. *Song of My People*. Dublin: Veritas Publications, 2002.

Reilly, Robert T. *Irish Saints*. New York: Avenel Books, 1964.

Sellner, Edward C. *Wisdom of the Celtic Saints*. Notre Dame, Ind.: Ave Maria Press, 1993.

NOTES
• • • • •

1. According to the writers of *Candlemas: Feast of Flames. Brigit's Festival of Light and Life*, Amber K. and Arynn K. Azrael, (St. Paul, Minn.: Llewellyn Publications, 2001), the saint's name is spelled "Brigid." The name of the goddess is "Brigit," from the Old Irish, and the name of in modern Gaelic is "Brighid," pronounced "Bree-id." However, because Brigit's powerful Threads of goddess, saint, and folk heroine became intimately intertwined over the centuries, this prayer service and companion essay will refer to her as Brigit, except in direct quotes regarding Saint Brigid. The book cited is hereafter referred to as Candlemas.

2. Catechumens are those who have never been baptized; candidates are those who have been baptized but have never celebrated the other sacraments of initiation, which are confirmation and eucharist.

3. See especially Galatians 3:26–28; this passage explicitly names the gospel relationships of Jesus.

4. From ancient times, it was recognized that that the complexity of divinity in a female figure, so intimately involved in the cycles of birth, life, and death, was best expressed in terms of a triple goddess. Artistically, this was rendered through the triple spiral, symbolizing cyclical regeneration and the never ending cycle of infinitude. And Brigit outshone all other triple-goddesses.

5. This prayer is adapted from a Celtic invocation to the Trinity for protection and guidance. Since St. Brigit forms a trinity of Irish sainthood in the hearts of the people, along with Saints Patrick and Columcille, this is an appropriate beginning. It is found in *The Celtic Vision: Selections from the Carmina Gadelica*, edited by Esther de Waal (Petersham, Mass.: St. Bede's Publications, 1988), p. 11, with a few additions from p. 104.

6. According to legend, her monastery produced the legendary but lost "Book of Kildare," not unlike the "Book of Kells."

"Until you have been clothed with power from on high."

7. Brigit was giver of the Brehon Laws, according to legend, the counterpart of the Torah.

8. Mary Condren, *The Serpent and the Goddess: Women, Religion, and Power in Celtic Ireland* (San Francisco: Harper & Row, 1989), 56.

9. Dubthach, meaning "the Dark One," is pronounced "Duffac;" Broicsech is pronounced "Brocksheh."

10. Edward C. Sellner, *Wisdom of the Celtic Saints* (Notre Dame, Ind.: Ave Maria Press, 1993), 70.

11. Ibid.

12. It is most appropriate that Brigit is born on February 1, breathing new life into the year's calendar, following immediately upon the "dead month" of January.

13. Sellner, p. 71.

14. Sellner, p. 72.

15. Ibid.

16. *Anecdota Oxoniensia*, "Life of Brigit," in *Lives of Saints from the Book of Lismore*, translated by Whitley Stokes, D.C.L. (Oxford: Clarendon Press, 1890), 188; hereafter referred to as *Anecdota*.

17. *Anecdota*, #1231, p. 185.

18. *Anecdota*, #1470, pp. 191–92.

19. *Anecdota*, #1759, p. 199.

20. Ibid., p. 200.

21. Ibid.

22. Galatians 3:28.

23. While this song is attributed to St. Patrick, it fits St. Brigit, as well, and reflects Celtic spirituality.

24. Condren, p. 56.

25. Candlemas, p. 23.

26. Sellner, p. 15.

27. Many rivers, for example, are named after goddesses. The Irish rivers Liffey and Shannon are named after the goddesses Life and Sinnann, and Brigit gave her name to the rivers Brigit, Braint, and Brent in Ireland, Wales, and England; see Condren, p. 27.

28. Condren, p. 57.

29. Condren, p. 60.

30. Condren, pp. 62–65.

31. Condren, p. 60. She credits Guy Ragland Phillips, *Brigantia: A Mystiography* (Boston: Routledge and Kegan Paul, 1976).

32. Some legends tell us that the Tuatha de Danaan are a branch of the Sidhe (pronounced "shee") or Good People. These are other-worldly, highly intelligent beings who include leprechauns and giants. In this capacity, Brigit became known as "Queen of the Faery" and "goddess of rulership" (Candlemas, p. 37).

33. Miranda Green, *Celtic Goddesses: Warriors, Virgins and Mothers* (New York: George Braziller Inc., 1995), 198, as found in Candlemas, p. 27.

34. Condren, p. 59.

35. The cow, in fact, was often associated with goddesses, symbolic of nurturing life.

36. Candlemas, p. 38.

37. Note that the cross of St. Brigit is surrounded by rays, as from the sun.

38. Condren, p. 58.

39. Condren, p. 65.

40. Nora K. Chadwick, *The Age of the Saints in the Early Celtic Church* (London: Oxford University Press, 1961), 2.

41. There were four major monasteries founded by women: Kildare (the most famous), Killeedy (founded by Ita), Killevy, and Clonbroney (founded by Samthann).

42. Ireland was rural, rather than urban, so monasteries assumed the role, usually performed by bishoprics, of organizing religious life. It is thought that the monastic tradition came to Ireland from the Coptic and Syrian traditions, probably through Aquitaine and Spain.

43. Sellner, p. 18.

44. Her ordination will be described in more detail in the next section on image of Christ.

45. Sellner, p. 27.

46. See Luke 1:26–38 and Matthew 1:18–25.

47. See Luke 3:23–38 and Matthew 1:1–17.

48. *Anecdota*, #1151, p. 183.

49. See Luke 2:25–40, for example.

50. *Anecdota*, #1192, p. 184; see Luke 7:11–17 (raising of the son of the widow of Nain from the dead) and Mark 5:35–43 (raising the daughter of Jairus to new life), also found in Matthew 9:18–26 and Luke 8:40–56, for example.

51. *Anecdota*, #1341, p. 188. Mary Condren offers another version of this story as she quotes from Broccán's Hymn, p. 65. The occasion was Bishop Mel's conferring the order of penitence on the nuns, but the outcome was the same.

"Until you have been clothed with power from on high."

52. Sellner, p. 71.

53. *Anecdota*, #1231, p. 185. See also John 2:1–12.

54. *Anecdota*, #1231, p. 185.

55. *Anecdota*, #1250, pp. 185–86.

56. *Anecdota*, #1755, p. 199. Compare with John 21:24–25.

57. John 19:31.

58. John 19:33.

59. Condren, p. 73.

60. See prayer service for an accounting of this.

61. Sellner, p. 16.

62. Lady Augusta Gregory, *A Book of Saints and Wonders* (London: John Murray, MMVII) as found on the Internet; a shorter version is found in Kathleen Hughes and Ann Hamlin, *Celtic Monasticism* (New York: The Seabury Press, 1981), 15.

63. Sellner, p. 74.

64. Esther de Waal, editor, *The Celtic Vision* (Petersham, Mass.: St. Bede's Publications, 1990), 9, quoted from the *Carmina Gadelica* I, 271, p. 83.

65. Chadwick, p. 71. This quote is taken from the eighth century document, *Catalogus Sanctorum Hiberniae* or *The Catalogue of the Saints of Ireland*. It describes three orders of saints, the first being the bishops, the "most holy." They were the ones who did not reject women.

66. Hughes and Hamlin, p. 8.

67. Ibid.

68. Sellner, p. 20, my emphasis.

69. *An Turas* means "the Journey" in Irish.

"Until you have been clothed with power from on high."

twelve

TERESA OF AVILA

We Are Set Free to Liberate Others

....

A Prayer Service Inspired by
Teresa of Avila

....

The environment is simple. The focus of the worship space is a table, on which is a very large stone and a green plant (or flowering plant). Next to the table is the Easter candle or other large candle. The musicians and cantor are on one side of this table and the leaders of prayer (leader, Teresa, and lector) are on the other. Chairs are in semi-circles, if possible.

Ministers: *leader, Teresa, lector, musicians, cantor*

Materials: *table, large stone, plant, Easter candle, chairs*

Gathering Rites

• •

CALL TO WORSHIP

• • • • • • • • • • • • • •

Leader: O, give thanks to the God of steadfast, enduring love.

All: Liberate us, O Christ, to live out of your gospel passion.

Leader: O, give thanks to the God of vulnerable risk taking.

All: Liberate us, O Christ, to live into your dangerous gospel.

Leader: O, give thanks to the God of mighty hand and outstretched arm.

All: Liberate us, O Christ, to live out of your powerful gospel.

Leader: O, give thanks to the God who is Emmanuel, God with us,

All: Liberate us, O Christ, to live with all your sisters and brothers

            as one family, in solidarity, integrity, courage, and joy.

Music of "Creator of the Stars of Night" softly begins as the leader continues:

Leader: Teresa was an ordinary woman. If someone had told her—at age twenty—all that she would ultimately claim as her vocation in life, she might well have scoffed. For she had backed into religious life and she knew it. She had joined the Carmelite convent of the Incarnation at age twenty-one to escape the "horror"—as she saw it—of marriage. And she was quite content, at first, to join in the lax, and even frivolous, environment in which she found herself. Add to that, she nearly died at age twenty-three and was paralyzed afterwards for nearly three years. Her health was

"Until you have been clothed with power from on high."

always in question. But, slowly, everything changed. In her mid-forties Teresa knew, without a shadow of a doubt, that God was calling her to reform the Carmelite order, to set it free to follow its original purpose of prayer and fasting, with great joy. In doing so, she would encounter nothing less than the ever-present Inquisition, which hovered—unlike the Holy Spirit—as a menacing bird about to devour its prey. And she would encounter the divisive opposition of those Carmelites who chose to stay in the Egypt of their comfort. A woman of wit, charm, courage, and profound faith, she points us along the path to freedom in God.

OPENING HYMN
. . . .

"Creator of the Stars of Night," text and tune from the ninth century Latin hymn *Conditor alme siderum*, acc. by Gerard Farrell, OSB, © 1986, GIA Publications, Inc.

Liturgy of the Word
. . . .

FIRST READING: WISDOM 10:9, 10:15–11:4.
. . . .

EXODUS 15, CANTICLE
. . . .

"I Will Sing to My God," text by Marty Haugen, based on Exodus 15, tune by Marty Haugen, © 1988, GIA Publications, Inc.

SECOND READING: ROMANS 8:18–19, 8:22–28.
. . . .

GOSPEL ACCLAMATION
. . . .

From *Mass of Creation*, verses 1, 2; text and tune by Marty Haugen, © 1984, GIA Publications, Inc.

"Until you have been clothed with power from on high."

Teresa of Avila

GOSPEL AND REFLECTION: MATTHEW 28:1–10

(by the lector and Teresa)

. . . .

Lector: After the sabbath, as the first day of the week was dawning, Mary Magdalene and the other Mary went to see the tomb (Matthew 28:1).

Teresa: I've been to the tomb. I know what it is to be dead, inside and out. I was young, and didn't know what I wanted out of life. I just knew I didn't want to marry. For I had seen men dominate their wives in all kinds of ways. And I had seen women worn out at a young age from bearing child after child after child. So, at age twenty-one, I entered the Convent of the Incarnation right here in Avila. It was congenial; there was plenty of time to visit with friends, men included. But then I became deathly ill. When I finally awoke, someone had even put the wax of death on my eyelids! It took me another three years to begin to recover, ever so slowly, for I was paralyzed. But I was given a book that I hungrily devoured, Francisco de Osuna's *Third Spiritual Alphabet*. And I began to turn to God, deep within.

Brief silence

Lector: And suddenly there was a great earthquake; for an angel of the Lord, descending from heaven, came and rolled back the stone and sat on it. His appearance was like lightning, and his clothing white as snow. For fear of him the guards shook and became like dead men. But the angel said to the women, "Do not be afraid; I know that you are looking for Jesus who was crucified. He is not here; for he has been raised, as he said" (Matthew 28:2–6a).

Teresa: My earthquake did not come all at once. It took time. Years of tilling the soil of my heart. Years of placing my vivid imagination, my sensual and outgoing nature at God's disposal. Years of turning to the God within, of even beginning with established prayers, like the "Our Father." Yet slowly but surely, I began to recognize that the stone of resurrection was being rolled

---

"Until you have been clothed with power from on high."

210   WALKING WITH WISDOM'S DAUGHTERS

away, from inside out. I began to know that prayer is "an intimate sharing between friends," making time "to be alone with him who we know loves us."[1] And Jesus, in his "sacred humanity" began to reveal such profound depths of his love for me!

I can still remember the Lent of my thirty-ninth year. I had come looking for the crucified Jesus . . . and found him in an earthquake. There were so many favors in prayer. Visions and voices, all from God. Transforming me. Setting me free to serve others. Rolling away the stone of resurrection, from inside out. It was as though someone had left me some jewels, making me very rich. And "I could show them these jewels—for all who knew me were well aware how my soul had changed . . . the difference was very great in every respect . . . such as all could clearly see . . . it was quite clear to me that these experiences had immediately made me a different person."[2]

Brief silence

Lector: "Come, see the place where he lay. Then go quickly and tell his disciples, 'He has been raised from the dead, and indeed he is going ahead of you to Galilee; there you will see him.' This is my message to you." So they left the tomb quickly with fear and great joy, and ran to tell his disciples. Suddenly Jesus met them and said, "Greetings!" And they came to him, took hold of his feet, and worshiped him. Then Jesus said to them, "Do not be afraid; go and tell my brothers to go to Galilee; there they will see me" (Matthew 28:6b–10).

Teresa: "Do not be afraid!" How often I needed to hear that! Remember; this was the time of the Inquisition. And I was a woman . . . with visions. And Jewish blood in my veins, besides. That alone would make me suspect. I still remember all those times when learned men would try to make me believe that my visions were the devil's work. As long as I was in prayer, I would never believe them. But, afterwards, "I was afraid, seeing who they were that spoke to me in that way, for I thought they must be speaking the truth, and that I, being who I was must be mistaken."[3] I was forty years old before I had a spiritual director who could really understand my spirituality. My dear friend, Peter of Alcantara, a Jesuit. Though by then, Christ himself had become my spiritual director. You see, the Inquisition had banned all our books, except those written in Latin. And most women, myself included, couldn't read them. Jesus appeared to me and said, "Don't worry Teresa. I will be a Living Book." He even taught me to question the men. "Tell them [he said] they should follow not just one part of scripture but they should look at other parts, and ask them if they can by chance tie my hands."[4]

Yes, it seems that I was to go and tell the others where Jesus was to be found. Not in the comfortable "mitigated" rule that my order had slipped into, but in the "Primitive Rule" of our twelfth century founders, a rule based on poverty, fasting, seclusion, and silence— and also joy, poetry, singing, and dancing. Certain of my mission, I began plans in my mid-forties to open the first of what would become seventeen reformed monasteries. But not without painful and divisive opposition, even from many of the Carmelites! I had to work in secret. And when I was forty-seven, Rome secretly approved San Jose, the first of these monasteries. In the end, our reform, the discalced—or shoeless—reform was set up in a separate province. And I spent years of difficult travel, always inspired by the words and vision of God for my life.

But this was never easy. My health was not good, and the weather was often frightful. I spent time in tumbledown and dirty houses, "put up with people of so many different temperaments in each place we visited" and was just plain homesick.[5] In the end, though, I was set free enough to even complain to God. The moment came not long before my death in 1582. The rain poured down in torrents, as it had often enough. The mule cart got stuck . . . one more time, one too many times! And I told God exactly how I felt about the whole thing! Then God said, "Do you not know

Teresa, that this is how I treat My friends?" "Well, if that's so [I said], then it's not surprising that you don't have many of them."[6] What freedom to be so honest! What freedom to be held in God's love!

Brief silence

PROCLAMATION OF MATTHEW 28:1–10 *(Lector)*
● ●

GOSPEL ACCLAMATION
● ● ● ● ● ● ● ● ● ● ● ● ● ● ● ● ● ● ● ●

From *Mass of Creation*, verses 3, 4, and 1.

Ritual of Freedom in God
● ●

INTRODUCTION
● ● ● ● ● ● ● ● ● ● ● ●

Leader: The ever human, ever irrepressible St. Teresa of Avila shows us what it means to be set free by God. She knew the desire for creature comforts . . . and the struggle to be faithful to prayer. She knew what it was to doubt herself and fear oppressive Church authority. And yet, because of God's overflowing fountain of grace from deep within and her daily persistence in following the "Sacred Humanity" of Jesus, she was set free to serve God's people. Others might call her foolish, but she knew the wisdom of God. And God transformed her very being, rolling away the stone of death, from inside out.

We, too, know the taste of death. Each of us. The too eager desire to please others, perhaps. Or the struggle to be faithful to God's call in the face of oppressive church authority. Or, something else. Please take a moment now to imagine yourself at the empty tomb. The stone is enormous! But it has been rolled away! (*Pause*) Allow yourself to be immersed in this moment of God's boundless love for you. What do you see? Hear? Feel? What fears, anxieties, doubts, death

"Until you have been clothed with power from on high."

experiences do you bring? What do you most need, in order to be set free, from inside out? (*Pause*)

When you are ready, come forward silently, touch the stone of your need (the large stone on the table) and then go to one of the leaders for a silent moment of prayer and blessing. You will then hear the leader say to you, as she lays hands on you in a gesture of healing, "May you be set free to serve God's people."

Coming Forward for Prayer and Blessing

The prayer leader, Teresa, and the lector each take a station across the front, waiting to pray silently with people and offer a blessing. This should not be rushed. During this time of reflection and silent coming forward, instrumental music will be played. Suggestions are as follows:

"Resucitó," text and tune by Kiko Arguello, © 1972, OCP Publications, © 1993, GIA Publications, Inc.

or

"O Sons and Daughters," text and tune O FILII ET FILIAE by Jean Tisserand (fifteenth century), translated by John M. Neale, acc. by Richard Proulx, © 1975, GIA Publications, Inc.

This might be concluded with one or two sung verses of one of these hymns.

Concluding Rites

Sign of Christ's Peace (*Initiated by the leader*)

COMMISSIONING

Leader: As you have been set free,

All: go and release others from the chains of fear.

Leader: As you have been transformed from inside out,

All:	go and become God's agents of change.
Leader:	Go, in companionship with St. Teresa of Avila,
	Go, assured of God's abundant power to roll away the stones of death,
	Go, in peace, courage, and the love of Jesus' "Sacred Humanity."
All:	Amen! Alleluia! Amen!

CLOSING HYMN
• • • • • • • • • • • •

"Daughters of Miriam," text and tune by Colleen Fulmer, from the cassette collection and book *Her Wings Unfurled*, © 1986.[7]

A Newspaper Account of the Life of Teresa of Avila
• •

Imagine that it is the sixteenth century . . . the year 1582 . . . the end of October of that year, to be precise. Imagine that you are living in the walled town of Avila, in what is today Spain. Imagine that you pick up the morning paper, over coffee, and are startled to read—even though many people cannot yet read—about the life and death of Teresa Sanchez. You know her, of course, as Teresa of Avila. She has just died, on October 15, to your great sadness. You know that she was one of ten siblings, born on March 28, 1515, to Alonso Sanchez and his second wife, Doña Beatriz de Ahumada. If you seek a more detailed autobiography, which can become a forty-five minute program, please check "Re-Mapping the Human Landscape" on the web site http://avemariapress.com/itemdetail.cfm?nItemid=780

Famous Daughter of the Church, Teresa of Avila, Goes Home to God

Many are mourning the death of the saintly Teresa of Avila on October 15, which will become forever known to many as her Feast Day. How can we possibly describe such a lively, holy, charming, strong-willed, persistent, brilliant daughter of the church? There are several names by which we know her. Mystic. Reformer of her order, known now as the Discalced (or Shoeless) Carmelites. Founder of seventeen monasteries in this reform movement. Church leader. Dear friend.

Avila is indeed proud to be home to this saintly mystic. Did our landscape inspire her prayerful account of her mystical relationship with the living God? Did our walled city, with its intermittent spires reaching to the heavens, give name to that remarkable book entitled *The Interior Castle?* We don't know. But we do know this. According to Teresa, "the soul of the just person is nothing else but a paradise where the Lord says he finds his delight."[8] Yes, the soul is like a crystal castle of seven rooms with Christ—"His Majesty"—at the center. How do we enter? Only with prayer, even the recitation of ordinary prayers like the "Our Father." Though, as Teresa pointed out, with her usual candor, there are pitfalls along the way. The devils will raise a terrible uproar, intended to detour our spiritual progress. But, she insisted, persistence and focus are the keys to unlocking these seven rooms.

Consider the life of Jesus. Collect "together all the faculties" and enter within "to be with . . . God," at your center.[9] And never forget that without your "guide [and mine], who is the good Jesus" in His "sacred humanity," we can never enter the final two dwelling places of spiritual marriage.[10] She knew that place so well! In one of her many visions, she saw an angel, with a long golden spear. "With this he seemed to pierce my heart several times so that it penetrated to my entrails. When he drew it out, I thought he was drawing them out with it and he left me completely afire with a great love for God."[11] With this fiery passion, Teresa would then often proclaim: the important thing in life "is not to think much, but to love much."[12]

But, Teresa didn't start out on this path. No, she backed into it, joining the Carmelite Convent of the Incarnation here in Avila at age twenty-one. As she later admitted, that decision resulted from her firm desire to avoid the pitfalls of marriage, including the threat of a dominating husband. Indeed, her father had earlier reined her in, from a compromising situation with one of her cousins, by placing her in the Augustinian convent, Our Lady of Grace, right here in Avila, as well. In any event, not long after her arrival at Incarnation, she became deathly ill, even paralyzed for three years. Her health would never be robust, but this would become a turning point, a turning to the God within.

And yet, it would take *years* before she found her other true vocation, reform of the Carmelite order, in line with its twelfth century roots. For many of the convents, hers included, had grown lax . . . departing from the original vision of poverty, fasting, seclusion, and silence. But this reform would never be easy. Teresa made enemies, both within and outside the convent. So, she needed to work in secret, and Rome secretly approved the first of these monasteries, San Jose, in another province. By this time, 1562, she was forty-seven years old. God's vision *always* kept her going, but *never* without difficulty. The weather was often terrible, her health never good, and she admitted to homesickness and to putting "up with people of so many different temperaments in each place we visited."[13]

Add to these difficulties, we must remember that this is the sixteenth century. And life for any woman, let alone a leader in the church, was trying, at best. She had her critics. The Papal Nuncio, Felipe Sega, said this: This Teresa of Jesus is "a restless, disobedient, stubborn, gad-about female who, under the guise of piety, has invented false doctrines, left the enclosure of her convent against the orders of the Council of Trent and her own superior, and has gone around teaching like a Doctor of the Church, contrary to the exhortations of St. Paul who said that women were not to teach."[14] As a woman, with visions, she was suspect. So many churchmen tried to convince her, early on, that her visions were from the devil and not from God. As long as she was in prayer, she never believed it. But, later, she would have doubts. As she put it, "I had enough troubles to drive me out of my mind."[15] Then there were all the rumors that Jewish blood ran in her veins, as well. Remember, in 1492, all Jewish people who chose not to become Catholic had to leave the country. Teresa's paternal grandfather stayed, spent a fortune defending himself against the Inquisition, and finally settled here in Avila.

And yet, she had friends who never gave up on her. Primary among them was Jesus. When the Inquisition banned all books except those written in Latin—and she, as a woman, could not read Latin—Jesus himself appeared to her, saying, "Don't worry, Teresa. I will give you a Living Book."[16] Then, of course, there was her dear friend, Peter of Alcantara, the Jesuit, who came to Avila in 1560. He became her spiritual director, and they became best friends. They . . . and we . . . give thanks for her courageous life! A life lived abundantly . . . faithfully . . . fruitfully . . . vividly . . . imaginatively . . . and uniquely.

SOME RESOURCES

. . . .

Galilea, Segundo. *The Future of Our Past: The Spanish Mystics Speak to Contemporary Spirituality*. Notre Dame, Ind.: Ave Maria Press, 1985.

Green, Deirdre. *Gold in the Crucible: Teresa of Avila and the Western Mystical Tradition*. Longmead, Shaftesbury, Dorset: Element Books Limited, 1989.

Gross, Francis L., Jr. and Toni Perior Gross. *The Making of a Mystic: Seasons in the Life of Teresa of Avila*. Albany: State University of New York Press, 1993.

Judy, Dwight H. *Embracing God: Praying with Teresa of Avila*. Nashville: Abingdon Press, 1996.

Lincoln, Victoria. *Teresa, a Woman: A Biography of Teresa of Avila*. Albany: State University of New York Press, 1984.

Luti, J. Mary. *Teresa of Avila's Way*. Collegeville, Minn.: Liturgical Press, 1991.

Slade, Carole. *St. Teresa of Avila: Author of a Heroic Life*. Berkeley: University of California Press, 1995.

Sullivan, John, O.C.D., ed. *Centenary of St. Teresa*, Catholic University Symposium, October 15-17, 1982. Washington, D.C.: ICS (Institute of Carmelite Studies) Publications, 1984.

Teresa of Avila. *The Interior Castle*. Translated by Kieran Kavanaugh, O.C.D. and Otilio Rodriguez, O.C.D. New York: Paulist Press, 1979.

_____. *Collected Works*. Trans. by Kieran Kavanaugh, O.C.D. and Otilio Rodriguez, O.C.D. Washington, D.C.: ICS Publications, 1987.

Teresa of Jesus, St. *Complete Works of Saint Teresa of Jesus*, 3 volumes. Translated and edited by E. Allison Peers. London: Sheed & Ward, 1946.

NOTES

· · · · ·

1. Teresa of Avila, *Life*, 8:5, as found in J. Mary Luti, *Teresa of Avila's Way* (Collegeville, Minn.: Liturgical Press, 1991), 87.

2. Teresa of Avila, *Life*, in *Complete Works of Saint Teresa of Jesus*, trans. and ed. E. Allison Peers (3 vols.) (London: Sheed & Ward, 1946) (I) 184–85, as found in Deirdre Green, *Gold in the Crucible* (Longmead, Shaftesbury, Dorset: Element Books Limited, 1989), 58.

3. Teresa of Avila, *Spiritual Relations*, in *Complete Works of Saint Teresa of Jesus* (I), p. 313, as found in Green, p. 163.

4. Teresa of Avila, *Spiritual Testimony*, p. 15, as found in Sonya Quitslund, "Feminist Spirituality in Teresa," in *Centenary of St. Teresa*, ed. John Sullivan, O.C.D. (Washington, D.C.: ICS Publications, 1984), 30; hereafter referred to as *Centenary*.

5. Teresa of Avila, *Book of Foundations*, in *Complete Works of Saint Teresa of Jesus* (III), p. 146, as found in Green, p. 25.

6. A legend about Teresa, found in Green, p. 31.

7. While this is an unfamiliar hymn, it is a perfect ending for this prayer service. It brings the liberation of God up to the present time and is a lively, easily learned hymn.

8. Teresa of Avila, *The Interior Castle*, trans. by Kieran Kavanaugh, O.C.D. and Otilio Rodriguez, O.C.D., (New York: Paulist Press, 1979), 35; hereafter cited as *Castle*.

9. Teresa of Avila, *Way of Perfection*, p. 115, as found in Deirdre Green, *Gold in the Crucible. Teresa of Avila and the Western Mystical Tradition*,

10. *Castle*, pp. 145, 146.

11. Teresa of Avila, *Life*, in *Collected Works* (I) 192-3, as found in Green, p. 45.

12. *Castle*, p. 70.

13. Teresa of Avila, *Book of Foundations* in *Complete Works of Saint Teresa of Jesus* (III), p. 146, as found in Green, p. 25.

"Until you have been clothed with power from on high."

14. Green, p. 153.

15. *The Life of Saint Teresa*, p. 81, as found in Green, p. 18.

16. Teresa of Avila, *The Book of Her Life*, 26, 5, as found in *Centenary of St. Teresa*, ed. John Sullivan, O.C.D. (Washington, D.C.: ICS Publications, 1984), p. 96, in an article by Ciriaco Moron-Arroyo, "'I Will Give You a Living Book': Spiritual Currents At the Time of Teresa of Jesus."

GLORIA ULTERINO, an active Catholic laywoman, is a preacher, storyteller, and leader of *"Women of the Well"* storytelling group in Rochester, New York. She has led the services in this book in parishes and retreat settings in western New York, at national gatherings such as the East Coast Religious Education Conference and Call to Action, and with various other groups since 1998. She holds masters' degrees in Divinity, Theology, and recent American History and is the author of numerous articles on pastoral ministry.

Enriching Woman's Spirituality

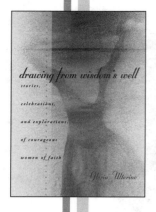

Drawing from Wisdom's Well
Stories, Celebrations, and Explorations of Courageous Women of Faith
Gloria L. Ulterino
Gloria Ulterino brings to life many women of faith in this extraordinary collection of communal celebrations. These celebrations involve us in the stories, the struggles, the hopes, and the deepest convictions of these amazing women of scripture and history.
Ideal for small faith sharing groups, retreat settings, and larger communal settings.
ISBN 0-87793-954-3 / 224 pages / $17.95 / Ave Maria Press

Rejoice, Beloved Woman!
The Psalms Revisioned
Barbara J. Monda
Barbara J. Monda reveals a new vision of the psalms, fashioned through the passionate and enlightened eyes and heart of a woman.
ISBN: 1-893732-80-0 /192 pages / $12.95 / Sorin Books

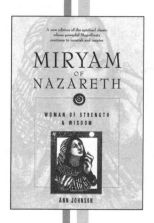

Miryam of Nazareth
Woman of Strength and Wisdom
Ann Johnson
Be enriched by the understanding of Mary as a Jewish woman and nourished by the Magnificats in a new edition of this classic of woman's spirituality.
ISBN: 0-87061-233-6 / 128 pages / $12.95 / Christian Classics

Available from your bookstore or from **ave maria press**
Notre Dame, IN 46556 / www.avemariapress.com
ph: 1.800.282.1865 / fax: 1.800.282.5681
Prices and availability subject to change.

Keycode: FØTØ5Ø6ØØØØ